What People Are Saying About *The Business of Cause Marketing*

"Rosica writes with graceful clarity, candor, and authority on cause-related marketing."

Walter Anderson, former Chairman and CEO of *Parade Magazine,* author of *Confidence Course,* and *Meant to Be*

"The importance of corporate social responsibility (CSR) as a marketing tool first began to be recognized in the 1960s. Today, cause marketing, a CSR extension, is permanently ensconced as a key element in many corporate success stories. Rosica has developed powerful cause-marketing programs for its clients for more than thirty years."

A.C. Croft, consultant to public relations firms, editor of *Management Strategies for Public Relations Firms* and author of *Managing a Public Relations Firm for Growth and Profit*

"Chris Rosica explores one of the most under–utilized techniques in marketing. Well written and convincing."

Al Ries, author of *Focus* and *The 22 Immutable Laws of Marketing*

"Rosica is a master at creating strategically smart marketing plans that position entrepreneurs for fast growth."

Verne Harnish, author of *Mastering the Rockefeller Habits: What You Must Do to Increase the Value of Your Fast-Growth Firm*

"Rosica continues to prove himself as the very best in the marketing industry. *The Business of Cause Marketing* is enormously insightful and a must-read for business leaders."

Brien Biondi—Former CEO of Young Entrepreneurs' Organization (www.eonetwork.org), *f*ormer executive director of Chief Executive Organization (www.ceo.org)

"The more you give, the more you get. Nowhere is this truer than in business. The companies which are truly devoted to doing good in the world also make a huge positive impact on their business. Rosica offers a compelling argument and clear guidance on turning good deeds into good strategy."

Simon Sinek, author of *Start with Why: How Great Leaders Inspire Everyone to Take Action*

"Rosica's experience in cause-related marketing provided us with valuable insight into this strategic PR practice. This helped us significantly with our Skate in School program, which is focused on fighting childhood obesity."

Nicholas Skally, Marketing and Public Relations Manager, Rollerblade USA

Advance Uncorrected Proofs
Pub Date 12/15/2011

The Business of Cause Marketing

Doing Well By Doing Good

by Christopher Rosica

Foreword by Wally "Famous" Amos

NOBLE PRESS

Published by Noble Press
Noble Press, 641 Lexington Avenue, 14th floor, New York, NY 10022, U.S.A.

Copies of this book may be purchased at:
www.CauseMarketingBook.com
Telephone: 866-843-5600

ISBN 10: 0-9793101-0-5
ISBN 13: 978-0-9793101-0-2

Cover design: Wendy Peters

Printed in the United States of America

For my parents, who taught me the importance of giving back, getting involved, and demonstrating compassion, and who also taught me how to forge powerful cause-marketing partnerships to positively impact the world.

Table of Contents

Table of Contents

The Business of Cause Marketing

Foreword

By Wally "Famous" Amos

When I started selling cookies in 1975, I had three things going for me: One was my aunt's cookie recipe, the second was a good attitude, and the third was a last name that rhymes with "famous."

But that was all I had: a good cookie, a good attitude, a good name.

A good start, perhaps, but it was barely enough to build a business. At least, not the kind of business I wanted. I lacked name recognition and, complicating matters, I had no advertising budget.

I did, however, have a good friend by the name of John Rosica, founder of Rosica Strategic Public Relations. In 1979, John introduced me to Literacy Volunteers of America (LVA). I had been looking for clever and novel ways to promote Famous Amos without spending money I did not have. At the time, LVA was a relatively unknown non-profit organization looking for a spokesperson to inform the public of its efforts to partner tutors with undereducated adults. Inspired by Rosica's vision, a partnership was born in the form of a groundbreaking cause-marketing effort.

Under Rosica's guidance, I became the spokesperson for Literacy Volunteers of America. Together, Rosica, LVA, and Famous Amos embarked on a promotional journey that bolstered recognition of our organizations nationwide and, at the same time, brought awareness to a major social problem: illiteracy. What happened was nothing short of tremendous. We enjoyed media coverage in newspapers, magazines, and on radio and television. Suddenly, our unknown companies were being covered in *People, Chicago Tribune, The New York Times,* and *Time Magazine.* Newscasters from *Good Morning America* and *The Today Show* were calling. Our promotional efforts enabled me to connect with then-First Lady Barbara Bush, who jumped aboard and began promoting literacy throughout the nation.

By 1985, only six years since forging its partnership with Famous Amos, Literacy Volunteers of America had increased brand recognition by 75 percent.

Who knew a chocolate chip cookie could be so powerful?

Today, I am blessed to still be a household name, lending credibility to the "famous" part of my name. I have guest-starred on sitcoms, developed into a paid speaker, and authored eight books. John Rosica and Rosica Public Relations played a major role in my success through our cause-related marketing effort with Literacy Volunteers of America.

While both LVA and Famous Amos gained a lot as a result of our partnership, it was the relationship we forged that meant the most to me. For nearly thirty years, I've been given the opportunity to advocate an important cause that is near and dear to my heart. And while it is one thing to have enjoyed professional success—and I know I have been truly fortunate in that respect—it is quite another to know that I have, at the same time, helped to change people's lives.

For that, I thank my dear friend John Rosica, a pioneer of cause marketing. Now, I look to his son, Chris Rosica, as the man responsible for continuing this legacy and helping to change the corporate and social climate through marketing programs that embrace education and responsibility. Inspired now by Chris' vision, your business can achieve its goals and, at the same time, effect change.

If a chocolate chip cookie can do it, so can you.

—Wally "Famous" Amos

The Business of Cause Marketing

Cause Marketing: What Is It?

Cause marketing, also referred to as cause-related marketing, is a public relations strategy that leverages the public's demand for socially responsible corporations by forging an alliance between a for-profit company and a non-profit organization (or "cause"). Under a cause-marketing campaign, a company incorporates a philanthropic agenda as part of its marketing strategy, garnering ongoing media attention and visibility through cause-related events, public relations activities, internal communications, merchandising, advertising, package design, online social media and marketing, and the like. Cause-marketing principles can be applied to any business model, whether the corporation is business-to-business or business-to-consumer, and regardless of company size.

* * * * * * * * *

The Business of Cause Marketing

Chapter 1:

The Case for Cause Marketing

A personal philanthropic effort used to be just that—personal. Prudent business owners ran tight ships and answered to stakeholders by pledging the most aggressive profit margin possible. If a business owner wanted to volunteer or donate to a charity, it was done in free time. Allocating corporate dollars or manpower to a charity would have been considered wasteful, inciting stakeholders to demand that the corporation restore a more conservative spending policy. Today, this is sometimes still true.

On the other hand, because they are currently threatened by consumers' increasing distrust of corporate America, an expansion of outsourcing to foreign countries such as China and India, a dire economy, and the lack of efficacy delivered by traditional marketing due primarily to information overload, corporations are now often looking for new strategies to substantiate and differentiate their brands, sustain their awareness, and actualize loyal customer followings. In turn, philanthropy has found a new home in the marketing efforts of corporate America. "Corporate social responsibility" has become a buzz phrase indicative of philanthropy's transition from personal choice to professional requirement. Cause-related marketing goes one step further.

In today's business climate, researchers have found a direct, positive correlation between corporate social performance and corporate financial performance.[1] Simply put, a corporation can increase its bottom line by increasing its philanthropic involvement, especially when economic factors leave companies anxious to bring in repeat and new customers. Countless studies corroborate these findings. A staggering 92 percent of Americans surveyed by Deloitte & Touche USA, LLP, think that charitable contributions in the form of dollars, products, or services from corporations to community non-profits are important.[2] When *PRWeek* revealed the outcome of its 2007 survey, no one should have been surprised by the results. Over 90 percent of consumers say it is important for companies to support causes and charities.[3] Another survey regarding price and quality found that 86 percent of Americans would consider switching from Brand A to Brand B if Brand B were associated with a worthy cause.[4]

Indeed, the face of the corporation—from small business to mega-chain—is changing. Or rather, it *has* changed. Businesses are no longer revered for curing society's ailments—they are charged with causing them. The word "corporate" is often paired with words like greed, scandal, or corruption. Big business, once lauded for providing countless jobs to blue-collar workers, is shamed for existing solely to turn a profit. Industries, once praised for breakthrough inventions, are fined for ruining the environment. Mega-chains are blamed for tarnishing a neighborhood's charm and character. And though a profit mindset can offer stability, create jobs, stimulate the economy, and contribute to a community's tax base, business people are nonetheless attacked simply for being profit-oriented.

This pervasive (though often cloaked) negativity toward business is just one obstacle which corporations face. Just as technology has trimmed costs and inflated production, it has also appropriated competition by creating fewer barriers to entry. The latest report from the U.S. Small Business Administration's Office of Advocacy shows that New Jersey alone has 750,000 small businesses, a calculation showing that approximately one in nine individuals owns a small business.[5] Due to advances in technology, this surplus of businesses means that companies must fight not only more and more neighboring competitors but also competition in Hawaii, Georgia, England, India, and China. And the corollary of increased competition? Yet another obstacle: Consumers and business customers are bombarded with ever-increasing numbers of marketing messages and gimmicks from companies urgently trying to secure their spot before a competitor sweeps in from Bangalore.

Significantly, most companies rely solely on traditional marketing to pursue their market share. Small businesses typically deem a professional logo, glossy pamphlet, and brochure-style website to be the staple of any reputable business. Medium-sized businesses embrace direct-mail campaigns, billboards, advertising, and some online media, while mega-corporations purchase airtime and invest in massive branding efforts by means of television, daily newspapers, magazine ad campaigns, and Internet marketing. Today, online businesses can profit from focusing primarily on Internet marketing strategies and tactics.

If traditional marketing is not dead, it is wheezing, fighting for each breath, and stabbed in the chest by digital video recorders, which have made television commercials nearly obsolete; spam filters, which have made e-mail marketing campaigns difficult to execute for even the smartest online marketers; and countless blogs and online media sites, which have put daily newspapers on life support. The inundation of marketing messages is evidenced by the countless billboards, online ads, coupons, postcards, newsletters, e-zines, blogs, brochures, and direct-mail pieces desensitizing both individual and corporate customers to the commercial message.

We simply cannot process all the commercial information hurled our way. Psychologist Mihaly Csikszentmihalyi believes that the five senses together are able to process, at most, only 126 of the two million bits—or less than 0.000065 percent—of information available each second.[6] Through necessity, we have been trained to perfect the art of selective filtering, tune out the advertisements, block our brains from processing one more piece of unnecessary information, avoid the commercial message, and focus only on the information we consider interesting and important. This is not to say that traditional and e-mail marketing campaigns never yield results, but rather that it is tougher than ever before to achieve results.

Many of the advertisements, postcards, commercials, pop-ups, and billboards are falling on deaf ears, but not for lack of trying. Corporate America continues to pump dollars into traditional and online marketing. Blackfriars Communications, a Massachusetts-based communication and research group, estimated that U.S. companies spent nearly $1.074 trillion in marketing in 2005. This represents about 9 percent of America's gross domestic product, ranking it fifth behind manufacturing, government, real estate, and professional services (if marketing were a vertical industry). In the second quarter of 2006, Blackfriars estimated that marketing dollars grew by 46 percent over the average quarter in 2005, a figure that includes online marketing.

Despite the ongoing growth in advertising dollars, most marketing experts agree that a consumer will fail to observe a commercial message until it has been presented at least five to eight times. And the likelihood that consumers will act on that message? The percentages are diminutive. The non-profit National Federation of Independent Business, which advocates for small and independent businesses, says that consumers are largely unwilling to consider a new product until they are "extremely motivated."[7]

Aggravating the challenges in disseminating commercial messages to a corporation's consumer or business clients is a collective and universally bad attitude toward sales. We consider salespeople to be inconsiderate and pushy, telemarketers the bane of our existence, and coupons and advertisements to be junk that is rudely (often without invitation) hogging space in our mailboxes and inboxes.

All of these indicators point to two giant hurdles. Not only is broadcasting a commercial message becoming exceedingly arduous, but the population is also weary of traditional marketing messages, which are struggling to produce those consumers who are "extremely motivated" to purchase a product or service.

Some companies have met these hurdles aggressively, deciding that "bigger and more often" is the solution to pumping success back into their marketing campaigns. If the competition sends a message ten times, they send it twenty times more frequently. Ignoring the importance of communicating the "right" message, they increase their marketing spending to the point of becoming pests, succeeding only in further annoying a great number of customers.

Still others turn to more modern and efficacious methods of marketing such as public relations, online marketing, and product placement for large companies; Internet-based marketing for medium to large businesses; and referral-based marketing for small businesses. Though these companies might succeed in achieving growth, they are missing an opportunity that, in combination with these efforts, could catapult their businesses to the next level and positively impact the perception of the company.

For a marketing campaign to reach the height of success, it must de-commercialize the commercial message. A business must take the sales out of the sales pitch and instead connect emotionally to its business and consumer-client base.

For a marketing campaign to reach the height of success, it must de-commercialize the commercial message. A business must take the sales out of the sales pitch and instead connect emotionally to its business and consumer-client base.

As discussed in my book, *The Authentic Brand*, if a company wants to build a brand, long gone are the days of hammering home the features and benefits of a product or service. In addition to offering a solid product, today's savvy corporations must also sell a "feeling" and connect with customers to stay competitive. They must recognize that today's consumer needs an emotional reason to buy a product. Harley-Davidson owners associate their motorcycles with freedom and American individualism. Apple Computers' users feel creative and hip. Consumers who purchase Newman's Own groceries feel charitably conscious. Ranger Boats, like Harley-Davidson, has crafted its image as all-American, and anglers feel pride in their brand selection.

Companies that embrace cause marketing use a new form of subliminal and image-altering messaging. They promote their commercial agenda indirectly by drawing direct attention to their good deeds and soliciting an honest response from consumers by appealing to their sensibilities and intelligence. Cause marketing leverages the public's desire for businesses to engage in socially responsible behavior, which has a twofold result. First, cause marketing furthers a philanthropic agenda, though the byproduct—the second result—is vital. If done properly, cause marketing engenders a feeling of "extreme motivation" in customers, convincing them to buy a product or service by communicating a positive feeling in addition to the commercial message.

Consider Microsoft. Beginning in the late 1990s and continuing through the turn of the millennium, the company faced an onslaught of public relations nightmares brought on by antitrust lawsuits that accused the company of unfair competition, predator pricing, and wielding monopoly power. The software giant was attacked for creating a popular product at a lower price than its competitors. Brought before the U.S. Justice Department, Microsoft was forced to "unbundle" its browser, Explorer, from its operating system, Windows. The scandal resulted in millions of dollars in legal fees. Though this caused only a dent in the company's short-term profits, it had significant long-term consequences. Microsoft's customer base, which had become increasingly reliant upon Microsoft's products, began resenting the company. Hearing tales of Microsoft's corporate greed, previously loyal customers began exploring other options. In doing so, they became increasingly reminded that it dominated the market, a fact that goaded the negativity directed toward the company.

Microsoft's brand seemed irrevocably tarnished. It was at a tipping-off point.

Microsoft's brand seemed irrevocably tarnished. It was at a tipping-off point. The company fought back by becoming a do-gooder. At the height of the lawsuits in 2000, CEO Bill Gates, along with his wife Melinda, created the Bill and Melinda Gates Foundation, which in 2006 was the largest charitable foundation in the world, "to help reduce inequities in the United States and around the world." (The word "inequities" might have been a clever strategy for combating the charge of unfair competition.) And despite legal fees in the tens of millions, the company more than doubled its charitable giving from $104.7 million in software and cash in the previous fiscal year to nearly $232 million, making it one of the top charitable corporations in the country in 2008.[8]

It was on its way to a rebirth in public perception.

Today, Microsoft has accomplished an about-face. Bill Gates is no longer viewed as a greedy corporate titan but is recognized as one of the nation's top entrepreneurs and philanthropists. In a 2007 survey by *PRWeek* and Barkely Public Relations, consumers and corporations both listed Microsoft as the company second-most committed to a charitable cause. Customers who purchase Microsoft's products know that they are supporting a company that stands for something more than profits. And it is no coincidence that the company's 2008 annual report listed more than an 18-percent increase ($9.30 billion) in revenues over 2007. Its reported operating income was up more than 21 percent, reaching a record of $22.49 billion. Despite increased competition from Apple Computers, Microsoft continued to demonstrate its commitment to giving back, and this commitment continued to pay.

In other words, the commitment is real and has shown real results.

Imagine the rebirth possibilities for oil companies if only they followed Microsoft's lead and, through demonstrated compassion and concern for the environment, convinced consumers that they are not the polluters their consumers believed them to be.

Cause marketing is a powerful but rarely seized opportunity for a corporation to strategically associate itself with philanthropic involvement and, in turn, to emotionally and intellectually connect with its existing and prospective customers. A pitiful five percent of charitable dollars are raised by corporations, a figure that demonstrates the need for corporate giving and points to a compelling reason for businesses to engage in cause-marketing partnerships.

Another case in point is Richard Branson. He combats the earth-unfriendly reality of running global airlines by seeking ways for jets to fly on alternative fuel. He feels that new technologies are smart *and* good business, and he has committed the Virgin Green Fund to investing $100 million in alternative energy.

Industrialist Henry Ford said, "There is but one rule for the industrialist, and that is: Make the highest quality goods possible at the lowest cost possible, paying the highest wages possible." This might have been the case during Ford's time, but I presume Gates and Branson would beg to differ. In today's market, businesses must wage a war against their rapidly deteriorating reputations by becoming philanthropists, by *doing good.* In turn, businesses will do well, achieving greater profits and decreased employee turnover. They will generate a solid image and good will while avoiding criti-

communications can be used to tell the story, such as merchandising, advertising, package design, online marketing, and the like, the greater the success will be.

Unlike corporate social responsibility, which often goes unnoticed (and might have a limited shelf life), a cause partnership is symbiotic, resulting in both ongoing elevated awareness and giving. *Cause marketing is a communications strategy and platform.* Corporations engaging in cause marketing disseminate good news to the world and to their network of influence, conveying through the campaign's key messages why the alliance is important, which in turn educates people about the charity and inspires outside involvement. Therefore, both the cause entity and the corporation partner in the storytelling process.

A true cause-marketing program helps both partners ward off competition. Competition is a particular threat to charities because of the great numbers of local aid organizations, legislation, and other occurrences such as natural disasters which may divert funds from one charity to another literally overnight.

Corporate social responsibility, on the other hand, is an expense that might benefit the global environment or community but lacks sustainability and high visibility—in all cultures, including corporate worlds, many good deeds go unnoticed and unrewarded—and falls short of inspiring individuals, communities, or nations to get involved to make an even greater impact. Corporate social responsibility does not help tell the non-profit entity's story, much less a business partner's story, and it does not typically have *ongoing* positive consequences. In addition, corporate social responsibility fails to improve customer loyalty or corporate profits, which can enable a company to make an ever-greater impact over time.

On the other hand, if executed wisely, cause marketing augments the charity's effectiveness and advocate base and at the same time enhances corporate profits, thus securing a win/win for both organizations.

Just look at what it did for the Susan G. Komen Foundation. This organization created an unparalleled support base because of the public relations it generated through many of its cause partnerships and the resultant media coverage. Today, throngs of businesses support breast-cancer research, especially during Breast Cancer Awareness Month, as we will discuss further in Step Two.

Social Entrepreneurship

Cause marketing also should not be confused with "social entrepreneurship," which is sometimes criticized as exploitative, though the jury remains divided on whether this condemnation is just. Though some are unethical and have been publicly scrutinized for misleading the public, most social entrepreneurs are skilled and savvy business people who use entrepreneurial principles to address a social problem, usually by streamlining a non-profit entity to run much like a business.

Social entrepreneurship is today's solution to the traditional model of non-profit groups wherein most employees, even those in directorial positions, lack the business tools and, occasionally, the know-how to succeed, further stressing the limited resources encumbered upon organizations that, by definition, cannot make a profit. This lack of know-how stems from the nature of the 501(c)3 model in which charitable organizations traditionally have been established and operated by constituents of the community served by the organization, a model that has proven to be problematic. The non-profit world is challenged in attracting and retaining talented people due to scaled-back compensation structures, restricted

Our results show that cause-marketing campaigns reach the height of their success when they are authentic, when their basis for existence is continuous and emotion-based in addition to being profit-based.

resources, and limited opportunities for advancement.

Under social entrepreneurship, a business person trained in the skills necessary to launch any organization—non-profit or otherwise—assigns business principles to increase donations and maximize impact in the same way he would increase profit and cut costs in a for-profit entity.

The last decade has seen the emergence of a new kind of social entrepreneur—one who creates a for-profit business that addresses a social problem. A casual onlooker of one such company might conclude that the company is a non-profit. Its mission statement, after all, says that the company helps the impoverished become economically self-reliant through financial services. Its website offers compelling stories about the destitute women in a third-world country who have been served by the company.

Yet the company is a for-profit entity. Though its client base *is* needy—it provides loans and insurance to disadvantaged women living in third-world countries—the company makes a profit from its products. To be sure, it may offer valid products, and some might even argue that its impoverished client base makes the company morally superior, regardless of whether it makes a profit. But the direct correlation between a needy client base and the company's bottom line makes this kind of social entrepreneurship a slippery slope. Though logic dictates that the company's clients would likely be worse off without the company's products, social entrepreneurs run the risk of being perceived as unethical businesspeople masquerading as social do-gooders.

Cause Marketing—A Smart Strategy

Under an effective cause-marketing program, the relationship between the cause and the company's bottom line is much more subtle than in the case of social entrepreneurship. Our results show that cause-marketing campaigns reach the height of their success when they are authentic, when their basis for existence is continuous and emotion-based in addition to being profit-based. As described by Phil Glosserman and Larry Pinci, co-authors of *Sell the Feeling: The 6-Step System That Drives People to Do Business with You*, consumers base buying decisions on emotions.[9] "Look at successful ad campaigns," wrote Glosserman and Pinci. "They're effective because they tap into the feelings that make people want to buy."

In *The Authentic Brand*, I also explore this concept, noting that if a company can sell the feelings associated with a cause, it will be more likely to pull at the heartstrings of its client base than a company that champions a cause *only* when the philanthropic effort presents an opportunity for the corporation to boost its bottom line.

Consider (PRODUCT)^RED^, the cause-marketing campaign created to raise awareness and money for The Global Fund, a charitable organization that helps women and children affected by HIV/AIDS in Africa. (RED)-branded products come from some of the world's largest companies, including Gap Inc., Apple Inc., Motorola, Emporio Armani, and Converse. During its first holiday season, (RED) products screamed at consumers from billboards on seemingly every street corner and in full-page advertisements in every major publication. Though they invested nearly $100 mil-

Strategic cause-related marketing goes beyond simply donating a percentage of a company's profit to a charity... strategic cause-related marketing is based on the premise that by doing good the company does well, as does the non-profit partner.

lion in advertising during their first year, promotional pieces quickly disappeared at the end of the holiday season, despite the general consensus that (PRODUCT)RED was far from meeting its philanthropic goals.

Not to worry—the campaign is anything if not opportunistic. As surely as the sun rises, (PRODUCT)RED billboards will flood our city streets when shoppers come out for the next holiday season. Recognized as opportunistic instead of genuine, consumers see that these campaigns only band-aid a problem instead of becoming truly involved in addressing a social ill.

For this reason, we advise against seasonal-based cause-marketing efforts, specifically those in which retailers donate a portion of sales to a charity. Christmas, Thanksgiving, Breast Cancer Awareness Month, and the like present opportunities for corporations to market themselves as philanthropic and boost sales with one-time advertisements or promotions. "Buy our product and help cure this social ill," the campaigns promise, as though consumers will believe that shopping can solve any disease, burden, or injustice. Consumers see right through these disingenuous tactics.

Results from outside polls show that consumers are more likely to purchase holiday gifts from stores that donate a percentage of their proceeds to a charity. Yet, the consumer is not fooled and considers these efforts to be underhanded, as evidenced by Rosica Strategic Public Relations' 2007 poll in which consumers were asked to rate the sincerity of a company that plans its cause-related marketing efforts to coincide with the holiday season. Nearly half (44 percent) of all consumers disparage this behavior as either entirely or mostly insincere. Seasonal and opportunistic strategies might reap short-term rewards, but with almost half of the population suspicious of their authenticity, these campaigns do little to promote a company's long-term brand equity and positioning. Rather, they instill even more distrust in corporate America than is already present. Today's consumer is smarter and savvier than ever before.

Another surefire strategy for a company to come across as disingenuous is to partner with a logical cause (such as a soup manufacturer whose cause partner is a soup kitchen). Again, the critical mistake made here is that the partnership seems contrived, and, though all corporations want to benefit from a cause partnership, showing a palpable profit motive will translate into increased distrust and a compromised brand, as discussed later in Chapter Two.

When embarked upon correctly and strategically, cause marketing is viral and guerilla-like in its marketing, addressing the emotional need of the customer to give back. Cause marketing generates excellent word-of-mouth marketing and delivers a strong return on investment. It also adds a refreshing human element that is not "salesy" by communicating that the corporate culture is compassionate and unique. And, as you are about to read, cause marketing can be a brilliant strategic move, even for those companies that object to the notion that "giving back" is their responsibility.

Cause Marketing—A Responsibility or a Strategy?

In today's corporate culture, companies are encouraged and often expected to give back, to embrace a philosophy of corporate social responsibility. And though corporate social responsibility is increasingly accepted by more and more consumers and corporations wanting to fight negative images, many businessmen and women (largely the free-market capitalists drawn to the appealing profit margin of a successful business) have yet to adopt corporate social "responsibility" as *their* obligation.

"There is one and only one social responsibility of business—to use its resources and engage in activities designed to increase its profits so long as it stays within the rules of the game, which is to say, engages in open and free competition without deception or fraud," wrote economist and future Nobel Laureate Milton Friedman over thirty-five years ago in *The New York Times Magazine.*[10] Friedman continued to defend this position until his death in 2006. As one of the best-known opponents of corporate social responsibility, Friedman repeatedly said that people who advocate corporate social responsibility are "preaching pure and unadulterated socialism."[11]

Others, of course, disagree, contending that the corporate world *should* assume responsibility for addressing social problems. Mainstream America agrees with this philosophy, declaring that because large corporations have huge resources, many of which they have obtained by exploiting the environment, they should devote some of their profits to addressing social issues.

The beauty of cause marketing is that it matters not whether you embrace corporate social responsibility as your responsibility. Cause marketing works and, though it incorporates socially responsible behavior, as previously mentioned, it is *not* the same. Strategic cause-related marketing goes beyond simply donating a percentage of a company's profit to a charity; it positions a social agenda as a platform for a marketing campaign, which has a positive domino effect. Cause marketing includes a strategic profit motive that even the freest market libertarians can embrace. After all, companies that incorporate cause marketing into their marketing and public relations strategy are rewarded with greater brand awareness, lower employee turnover, and increased profits, all of which benefit the stakeholder, an outcome that can surely be championed even by the Milton Friedmans and Henry Fords of the world.

Strategic cause-related marketing goes beyond simply donating a percentage of a company's profit to a charity. While corporate social responsibility often focuses on doing good simply for the sake of doing good, strategic cause-related marketing is based on the premise that by doing good (and telling the good news), the company does well, as does the non-profit partner.

Progressive business owners, consumers, and stockholders appreciate the advantage of cause marketing's effect on consumer buying habits. One recent study shows that nearly 80 percent of people are more likely to buy from a corporation that supports a non-profit organization,[12] so even if a company doesn't get the "warm and fuzzy" feeling associated with *doing good*, it surely enjoys the bottom line that comes along with these activities. That a company's cause-related marketing efforts also help better the world, or community, is "gravy" (for those who argue in favor of corporate social responsibility) or irrelevant (for those who argue that corporate social responsibility is not their responsibility).

"There can be little doubt that a certain amount of corporate philanthropy is simply good business and works for the long-term benefit of the investors," wrote John Mackey,[13] founder of Whole Foods. Mackey created "5% Days" to introduce new shoppers to the store, increase revenues, and support non-profit organizations. On these designated days, each Whole Foods grocery store donates 5 percent of its total sales to specified non-profit organizations. They select the non-profit entities in part by their number of donors, who are contacted and encouraged to shop at Whole Foods on these promotional days, thereby supporting their cause and increasing profits for the company. While donating a percentage of sales is a common approach, and more creative partnerships can be formed (as we will explore later in this book), Whole Foods created a loyal customer following, as well as a proud employee base, through this effort. While the company's sincerity and motives have been scrutinized, Whole Foods' cause-marketing effort is a good example of the "win-win" scenario established by cause partnerships.

* * * * * * * * *

An Effective Cause-Marketing Campaign Sees Five Wins in One

First Winner: The Company

As previously mentioned, a carefully established cause-marketing campaign helps a company increase sales, build brand awareness, improve employee morale, and create fresh publicity strategies. As well, it is a strategic move that can limit or help manage internal or external crises.

Second Winner: The Cause

Through the cause partnership, the non-profit organization builds greater awareness among all its key influencers and in the community. It enjoys more resources in terms of donations and volunteers, and it benefits from the corporate know-how of a successful business. Not coincidentally, it is this same "know-how" that led Warren Buffett, the second richest man in the world, to donate a giant chunk of his $44 billion Berkshire Hathaway fortune to the Bill and Melinda Gates Foundation. Buffett's announcement in June 2006 was accompanied by an explanation that a charitable foundation created by the founder of Microsoft would surely have the knowledge and ability to properly manage his donation.

Third Winner: The Customer

Whether an organization is a business-to-business or business-to-consumer company, its customer base is able and willing to support a cause while conducting its everyday business. In this fast-paced environment, consumers typically do not have the time, money, or energy to volunteer their efforts or resources to a charity. Through cause marketing, consumers can rest assured that they are doing good when doing business with corporations that support causes. In fact, according to a recent study, 86 percent of consumers are likely to switch from one brand to another if the brand is associated with a cause.[14] And the same study shows that nearly three quarters of the population, particularly women (who are also the primary target audience of nearly every consumer-product company, since women tend to make a household's purchasing decisions) *prefer* to do business with socially responsible companies.

Fourth Winner: The Employee

By participating in a company's cause audit (See Chapter Two), employees become emotionally engaged and are able to support a cause while at work, therefore making their jobs more fulfilling. Like consumers, employees are able to fulfill their philanthropic responsibilities while doing double duty, as both an employee of the for-profit company and a volunteer for the non-profit organization.

Fifth Winner: Society

Through this positive contribution, the company helps promote a social agenda, generating good will in a move that is certain to impact society for the better.

* * * * * * * * *

Notice that when the customers and employees benefit, the corporation concurrently reaps rewards. By making a business more desirable to the consumer, the business's bottom line is improved. Moreover, when an employee finds his/her job more fulfilling, the company is rewarded with greater productivity and less turnover.

For those skeptics who remain unconvinced of the benefits of cause marketing, let's look at the top five reasons why companies engage in cause-marketing campaigns.

Reason #1: To Bolster Sales

When properly implemented, cause marketing attracts media attention, which gives the public greater awareness of the company. And greater publicity (especially positive publicity) always translates into a bigger bottom line and desirability factor. A company that engages in a cause-marketing campaign enjoys increased sales because consumers show a greater interest in conducting business with charitable corporations. Because cause-related marketing impacts a company or brand's image, it also impacts customer loyalty, which means that a company sees repeat sales from its existing client base and attracts new ones.

A company's cause-marketing efforts prove the old adage that "the more you give, the more you get." Case in point: The Aspen East Fitness and Well Being Center and its principal, Steve Garrigan, wanted to boost awareness in the media to increase membership and boost the personal training division. To do this, the small business engaged in a cause-marketing partnership with the Spina Bifida Research Foundation. After just one highly successful media event, the fitness center saw a 30-percent increase in quarterly sales, pumped up by a 27-percent increase in its personal training business.

Reason #2: To Build Brand Awareness

Did anyone outside of Los Angeles and New York City know Famous Amos Cookies before it partnered in the 1970s with Literacy Volunteers of America, another little-known brand? Without its cause-marketing partnership with LVA, would the company's brand have eventually been purchased by Keebler? Probably not. After all, Famous Amos Cookies began with no advertising budget whatsoever. However, in a textbook case that is still studied in college marketing classrooms today, Famous Amos and LVA partnered to develop grassroots media events that spread the message nationwide. With the help of Rosica Mulhern & Associates and its founding partners, Bill Mulhern, Marilyn Rosica, and John Rosica, the team built brand awareness for Famous Amos Cookies, which eventually was purchased for millions.

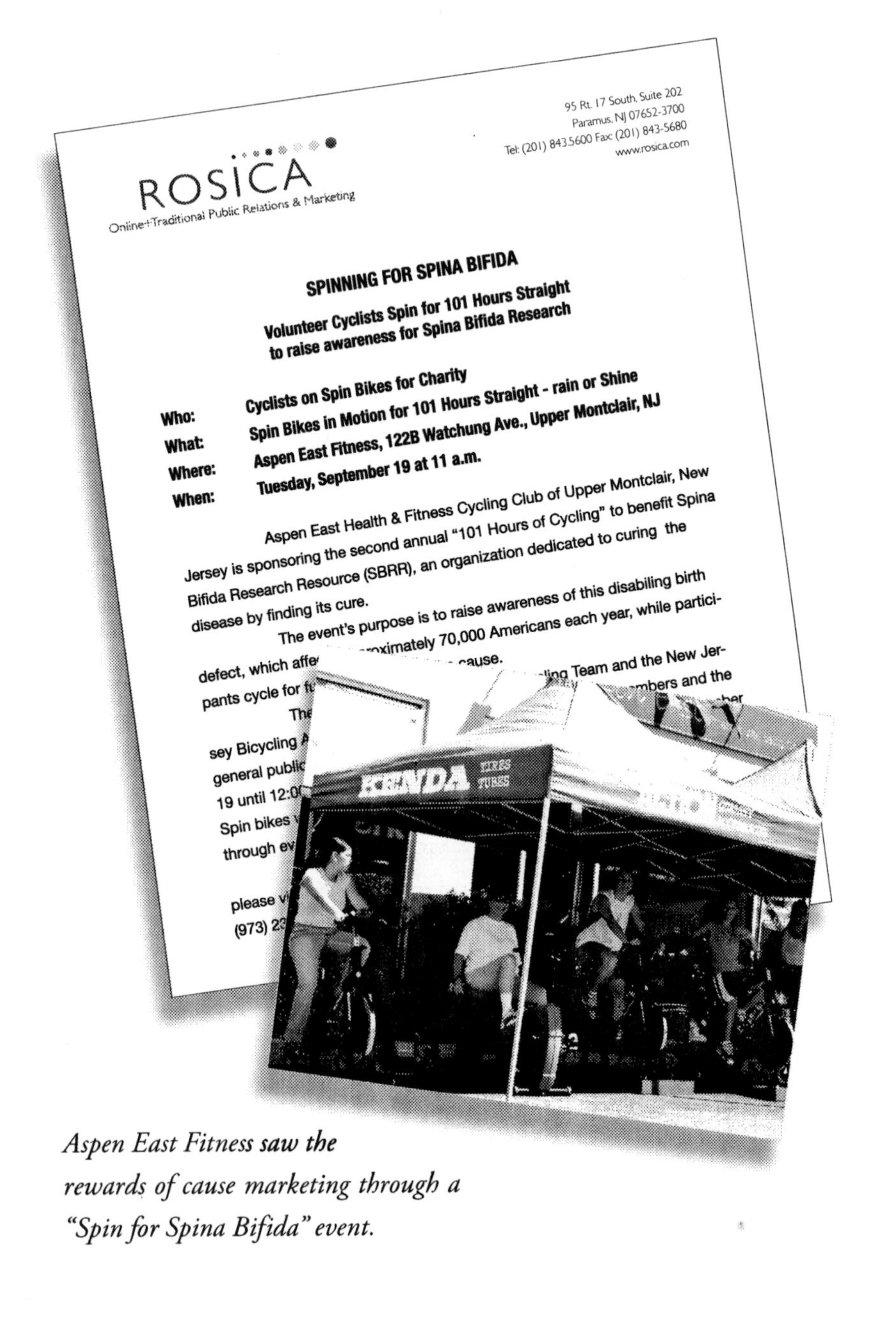

95 Rt. 17 South, Suite 202
Paramus, NJ 07652-3700
Tel: (201) 843.5600 Fax: (201) 843-5680
www.rosica.com

ROSICA
Online+Traditional Public Relations & Marketing

SPINNING FOR SPINA BIFIDA

Volunteer Cyclists Spin for 101 Hours Straight to raise awareness for Spina Bifida Research

Who: Cyclists on Spin Bikes for Charity
What: Spin Bikes in Motion for 101 Hours Straight - rain or Shine
Where: Aspen East Fitness, 122B Watchung Ave., Upper Montclair, NJ
When: Tuesday, September 19 at 11 a.m.

Aspen East Health & Fitness Cycling Club of Upper Montclair, New Jersey is sponsoring the second annual "101 Hours of Cycling" to benefit Spina Bifida Research Resource (SBRR), an organization dedicated to curing the disease by finding its cure.

The event's purpose is to raise awareness of this disabiling birth defect, which affe[...]oximately 70,000 Americans each year, while partici-pants cycle for fu[...] cause.

The [...]ling Team and the New Jer-sey Bicycling A[...]mbers and the general public [...]

19 until 12:0[...]

Spin bikes [...]

through ev[...]

please v[...]

(973) 2[...]

Aspen East Fitness saw the rewards of cause marketing through a "Spin for Spina Bifida" event.

Reason #3: To Improve Employee Morale

Companies that face high employee turnover and demoralized employees can ignite their employees' passions by engaging in cause marketing. Common sense dictates that happier employees are more productive employees. If employees feel deeply passionate about a cause and understand that the company is concerned with more than profits, the company will see greater productivity and lower turnover. Companies that engage in cause-marketing campaigns will witness the entire corporate culture change for the better. Employees, excited about going to work, will feel good about the work they do. In turn, the company's bottom line will increase. It will also attract higher-quality employees. A study by Roper Starch Worldwide and Cone, Inc., found that 85 percent of companies surveyed reported that support of philanthropic activities increased employee loyalty; 82 percent said that by aligning themselves with causes, they became more desirable employers.

Reason #4: To Manage or Avoid Crises

In a perfect world, cause marketing should be proactive. Optimally, it should begin long before a company faces a public relations crisis, so that if and when an obstacle presents itself, the company has already established itself as a charitable one, and the fallout is not devastating. But let's face it—many companies turn to public relations only as a solution to a crisis.

Consider our client African Pride, the makers of hair and skin products for the multicultural marketplace. Facing a boycott by the African-American community, African Pride had to act quickly. When African Pride enlisted our help, we partnered it with the Birthing Project USA, a non-profit organization devoted to saving babies' lives in underserved and disadvantaged communities.

African Pride was able to gain nationwide recognition as the corporate partner of this worthy cause. The organization grew to fifty chapters across the country, and the negative publicity for African Pride was long forgotten. The company's sales exploded, as did its brand equity. In fact, African Pride's visibility was so favorable that Revlon later purchased it.

Reason #5: To Create a Fresh Public Relations and Publicity Strategy

One of a company's main challenges is to keep itself fresh in the minds of its audiences when the company has nothing new to report. Ongoing media attention helps corporations (both business-to-business and business-to-consumer) build their brands by providing third-party endorsements, thereby boosting credibility and visibility. Cause marketing gives a company an evergreen story to tell. In terms of public relations coverage, this practice keeps the momentum going; it keeps the spotlight on the company *year-round.*

Cause marketing gives a company an evergreen story to tell. In terms of public relations coverage, this practice keeps the momentum going; it keeps the spotlight on the company *year-round.*

No one knows the power of a proactive cause-marketing campaign better than Stew Leonard's, a Connecticut dairy farm and retail store that later became a chain. Even though the day-to-day happenings at the store were rather mundane, we helped Stew Leonard's garner hundreds of millions of favorable media impressions by engaging in a year-round promotion with non-profit organizations, including a "wishing well" whereby customers' donations were matched by the store.

As a result, Stew Leonard's saw a 29-percent increase in sales during the first year of the campaign. Today, the chain is the world's largest dairy store and recently earned a spot on *Fortune* magazine's annual list of the "100 Best Companies to Work For." While we do not condone its later actions, the company not only survived a tax crisis but also continued to thrive, due in large part to its cause/community-centric approach.

* * * * * * * * *

My philosophy, inspired by my father, is that nearly every company, regardless of size or objectives, should incorporate cause marketing into its public relations strategy. Not only do we know that our clients (80 percent of whom are engaged in some aspect of cause marketing) benefit from cause marketing, but we also know they set themselves apart by partnering with charities. According to a July 2006 article in *Newsweek*, only 5 percent of charitable donations come from corporations. Clearly, much opportunity exists for companies to engage in strategic cause marketing and establish themselves as philanthropic leaders. And although a Conference Board survey found that 51 of 77 large North American corporations said that using philanthropy to further their business goals was one of their top three priorities,[15] actions speak louder than words. Most companies fail to disseminate their commercial message through cause partnerships. Instead, they rely on traditional forms of marketing that do little to differentiate them.

Those that do embrace cause marketing most often go about it in the wrong way. They do not know how to select a strategic cause partner and fail to "own" a cause in their customers' minds. They typically select an obvious charity, one that makes too much sense, and then wonder why consumers do not pay attention and/or think the partnership is disingenuous. They try to align themselves with one of the top charities, mistakenly thinking that the bigger the cause the better the result, overlooking the fact that they will be overshadowed by the nationally known charity. Or, they decide to work with many different causes, thinking that involvement with a variety of causes will get them noticed or produce a more favorable outcome.

These common mistakes, which unfortunately are often made by internal marketing departments or even top leadership, are caused by a lack of experience in executing strategic cause-related marketing campaigns. Soon, we will explore why the best partnerships are those that occur between a corporation and an *up-and-coming* non-profit entity and why it is important for businesses to limit the number of charities with which they partner. While the "more the merrier" might be true of a party, it is not true when it comes to smart cause-marketing campaigns. Partner relationships that do not immediately make sense can actually lead to the best results, while those that make too much sense might be considered "cutesy" and disingenuous (such as Wishbone Dressing's partnership with Make-A-Wish Foundation). Today's savvy consumers question these relationships and their perception can make or break a brand's future.

* * * * * * * * *

To most effectively form a partnership and garner media attention, we take our clients through the following five-step process, as detailed in each subsequent chapter of this book.

Step One: Identifying Your Objectives

In this step, we walk through a process that helps identify *why* companies want to engage in a cause-marketing campaign.

These objectives drive a cause-marketing campaign and often the rest of a marketing plan. For instance, if a business needs to manage a crisis, the cause-marketing campaign effort might look different from one that purports to increase employee morale. If this is the case, employee morale may come first—before publicizing the business, its founders, successes, products, or employees. By identifying objectives, businesses also identify specific and measurable outcomes.

Step Two: Conducting a Cause-Marketing Audit and Selecting a Cause Partner

In Step Two, we will provide a process for uncovering potential charitable organizations that their companies can get behind. This step focuses on gathering feedback from key players (management, employees, partners, board, investors, etc.) so that the chosen cause is one that employees can support and embrace. It provides a series of questions that can be used to solicit feedback from a team. As well, Step Two provides criteria for choosing a cause (for instance, choosing a cause that can generate media-friendly photo opportunities).

Note that we are not condoning decision by committee, as explained in detail later. Ultimately, the CEO or other top executive, in concert with the company's cause-marketing counsel, should make the decision and select the cause partner. However, by simply listening to team members, a CEO or executive can build morale and generate enthusiasm among the ranks. This may be the key that unlocks the door to finding a charity that resonates and engenders passion.

This step also helps companies select the *right* cause partner. We will explain in detail why pairing up with mammoth causes can be challenging, why it is best to choose an illogical match, and how and why it is best to find up-and-coming causes. This step also reveals how to approach a cause partner and evaluate the potential collaboration.

Step Three: Establishing the Cause Partnership

This step focuses on structuring the relationship with the nonprofit entity by identifying elements of a successful partnership and discussing the details necessary to negotiate terms so that both entities meet their objectives.

Step Four: Developing a Plan, Creating a Timeline, and Implementing the Cause-Marketing Campaign

Step Four helps identify the key ingredients of a cause-marketing campaign, as well as clarify and divide responsibilities. Readers put their ideas to work and start enjoying the benefits of the cause-marketing campaign, learning how to make the most of the effort and how to garner media coverage.

Step Five: Measuring Results

In the final step, tools are provided to measure the results of a cause-marketing campaign specific to each objective identified in Step One. You will learn how to maintain a successful cause-marketing partnership, what to expect from it, and what to do if the collaboration is not working.

* * * * * * * * *

The effect is that a company's bottom line will surge with a successful cause-marketing effort. By embracing the key principles described herein, businesses will do good and, as a result, will do well.

Chapter 2:

Identifying Your Objectives

With all of its charitable sentiment and seeming good will, a cause-marketing partnership is mistakenly considered by many to be nothing more than a philanthropic endeavor, the byproduct of advocates of corporate social responsibility. The corporation determines that by bestowing money upon a worthy cause, donating a percentage of proceeds, or contributing goods to a cause, it can fulfill its humanitarian quota for the day and move on to more important and strategic business matters.

This might have been the case when big business started involving itself in corporate giving. When American Express partnered with the Statue of Liberty Restoration project in 1983, it did little more than donate one penny toward restoring Lady Liberty for every American Express transaction made. The partnership received rave reviews, and, although cause marketing had been around for several years prior (both Famous Amos Cookies and Ben & Jerry's were already deeply entrenched in cause-marketing campaigns), the American Express/Statue of Liberty Restoration collaboration brought charitable marketing agreements into mainstream corporate America.

Corporations that participate in such partnerships are going through the motions, but consumers are not engaged and often learn of these partnerships only through advertisements... Consumers are, at best, bored...and, at worst, skeptical...

Today, such arrangements are commonplace. Panera Bread, a Missouri-based chain of bakery-cafes, donates its unsold bakery products each day to a local food bank. The Gap, Motorola, American Express, Converse, Apple, and Emporio Armani are just a few of the mega-corporations signed on to help the (PRODUCT)^{RED} campaign, founded to benefit The Global Fund to Fight AIDS, Tuberculosis, and Malaria. During Breast Cancer Awareness Month, BMW donates $1 to the Susan G. Komen Breast Cancer Foundation for every mile that consumers test-drive BMWs. Firehouse Subs, a Florida-based chain of sandwich franchises, is one of thousands of companies asking its customers to donate $1 to its pet charity (in this case, the Muscular Dystrophy Association). Target donates a percentage of its sales to select children's charities during the holidays.

Though this category of corporate giving certainly advances the cause it backs, it has become too routine to offer much in the way of supporting the corporations championing the causes and creating a larger impact. Corporations that participate in such partnerships are going through the motions, but consumers are not engaged and often learn of these partnerships only through advertisements (fully funded by the company and viewed as self-serving).

Consumers are, at best, bored with this class of philanthropy and, at worst, skeptical of corporations which engage in them. In some cases, the concern seems manufactured and half-hearted. Perhaps the flaw of (PRODUCT)RED is that it equates an end to human suffering with shopping. The campaign suggests that if only consumers would buy more (RED)-branded products, AIDS, tuberculosis, and malaria would end. No wonder the campaign was criticized for taking so long to generate results! Though expected to raise massive amounts of money for The Global Fund, the project failed to justify the cost outlay its participants incurred during its first year, raising only $18 million. This might seem like a lot of money, but think again. The massive billboard and print advertising campaign its major corporate sponsors implemented was estimated to cost at least $100 million. Consumers are critical and cynical of this tactic for good reason. Instead of spending $100 million on billboards, why didn't the companies simply donate to The Global Fund?

A truly effective cause-marketing partnership is much more strategic, because its authenticity, goal-driven nature, and profit motives are less transparent than the (PRODUCT)RED campaign. Instead of simply giving a percentage of sales to a charity, the most advantageous cause-marketing programs outline both the cause and the corporation's objectives and then create a strategic communications program that tells the story of the partnership. These collaborations generate extraordinary outcomes—especially during a recession—because they emotionalize the company's relationship with a charity, an outcome that transparent and strictly ad-driven campaigns are lacking. A true cause partnership is not at all the cookie-cutter model onto which most businesses have latched, succeeding only in providing temporary fixes by donating a percentage of sales or profits to a worthy cause.

Instead of simply giving a percentage of sales to a charity, the most advantageous cause-marketing programs outline both the cause and the corporation's objectives and then create a strategic communications program that tells the story of the partnership.

Identifying, understanding, and outlining the goals of both the non-profit and the for-profit entities up front lead to better partnerships that create the impression of a wide gap between motive and profit. By taking extra time in the beginning stages of a cause-marketing effort to nail down the specific intentions and opportunities of the collaboration, a corporation and its non-profit partner can avoid potential misunderstandings and obstacles.

Most companies jump right into their cause-marketing campaign without going through a fundamental process to help them identify the guidelines that will determine the campaign's success.

Most companies jump right into their cause.

As business people, we know the importance of sales goals and bottom-line objectives. In fact, this step might seem sophomoric in its simplicity. Consequently, most companies skip right over it. They assume their objectives are obvious, and they jump into their cause-marketing campaign without going through a fundamental process to help them identify the guidelines that will determine the campaign's success. If you do not know where you are going, any road will take you there. In other words, without identification of the endpoint, there is no telling what outcomes a cause-marketing partnership might see. By identifying these goals prior to launching a cause-marketing campaign, a company can define the target activities and efforts necessary for achieving them.

This chapter explains five corporate objectives that cause marketing can help a company realize. This chapter also discusses how the right partner can complement these objectives and, conversely, how the wrong one can challenge them. Through this process, readers uncover outcomes that they might have otherwise overlooked.

When our firm's clients first approach us, they usually have an immediate problem, need, or goal that requires attention. Before we do anything, we take them through a fact-finding process that, without fail, helps them recognize other priorities. When pressed to contemplate long-term goals, our clients discover other objectives necessary to their success, such as the creation of a succession plan or increased margins through heightened employee productivity, both of which can be supported through cause marketing. Though one objective might be the most pronounced—a company might need to manage a pending crisis or want to better position itself for acquisition—going through the objective-setting process helps a company recognize the secondary or tertiary goals that go hand-in-hand with its primary objective. As an outcome of a pending crisis, for instance, employee morale might be at an all-time low or turnover of key staff at an all-time high. The company, therefore, would add "increase morale" to its objectives.

We know that our clients (and readers of this book) will uncover ancillary goals by going through an intentional objective-setting process. They become clearer as to why they are engaging in a cause-marketing campaign, and they discover all of the benefits that a cause-marketing program has to offer—and they are plentiful. So even if you think you have already accomplished this step, the campaign will be most successful if it begins with an intentional objective-setting process that identifies what you hope to achieve from your cause-marketing partnership.

These findings will then drive your campaign. You will refer to these goals with each decision you make, guiding your cause audit (Step Two) by allowing you to evaluate employee interests as they might complement or detract from your overall goals. These priorities will then help you evaluate and ultimately choose your cause partner (Step Three). If your objective is to improve brand awareness and your cause partner needs to maintain a low profile to protect the identity of the community it serves (for instance, battered women), you are unlikely to have a successful media relations effort.

Your objectives will be particularly critical during Step Four, at which point you will begin implementing the campaign. When mapping the events of your cause-marketing campaign, your public relations agency partner or internal public relations staff will brainstorm effective strategies to garner traditional and online media coverage and help you achieve your goals through communicating *targeted messages* to your audiences. You can help narrow down your choices by constantly asking yourself the following question: *How does this activity drive our objectives?* If you seek to improve employee morale, for instance, you will be more inclined to select cause-related activities that engage your people.

Ultimately, your objectives will help you measure results (Step Five). These goals will serve as the standard by which you determine whether your cause-marketing campaign is a success, or whether it needs to be altered.

For-profit partner objectives are formed on a case-by-case basis; however, they most often fall into one of the following categories:

1. Increasing sales
2. Increasing brand awareness and brand equity
3. Improving employee morale
4. Preventing or managing crises
5. Creating a fresh publicity strategy

By considering each of these categories and comparing them to the company's overall business objectives, a corporation is often awakened to new possibilities. While some CEOs understand that cause marketing can help increase brand recognition, few recognize how a successful program can impact employee morale. In essence, a business will identify new objectives by reading through a short description of these five groups.

Objective #1—Giving and Getting: Cause Marketing as a Tool for Increasing the Bottom Line

By dedicating hundreds of pro bono hours to charities each year, we have based our entire company on the idea that the more you give, the more you get. Some call this karma; others call it justice. If you do good things, says karma, good things will happen to you. What goes around, says justice, comes around.

If you do good, we say, you can also do well.

Ultimately, "doing well" is the reason most companies consider engaging in a cause-related marketing campaign. Despite their desire to engage in corporate giving, most business-people still hold sacred the notion that boosting sales and increasing the profit margin are their first responsibilities and are musts for the company to sustain its employee base, survive increased competition, and combat the economic recession that has left many companies fighting for survival.

Still, increased sales usually go in tandem with other goals. The natural outcome of a cause-marketing campaign is a trickle-down effect in which the campaign influences the bottom line and more. A company might want to improve employee morale in an effort to improve the bottom line; by improving morale, the entire corporate culture of a company will change. As employees start finding meaning in their jobs, they will become more productive. Another company might want to avoid a crisis to protect its bottom line, so it strengthens its brand by engaging in a cause-marketing effort. In turn, the corporation receives heightened visibility, is recognized for its compassion, and is better positioned for acquisition. The bottom line improves not only because the crisis was averted but also because the company came away with a better reputation. You get the point. Any cause-marketing campaign is bound to result in increased sales and profits due to the improved customer loyalty factor, even if sales is not the primary goal.

Increasing revenues is the primary outcome for most corporations that engage in cause-marketing campaigns.

The beauty of cause marketing is that it enables a company to "de-commercialize" a commercial message and still benefit from an increased bottom line. Ostensibly, a for-profit business and a non-profit group have diametrically opposing relationships with money. The public considers a for-profit company to exist simply to make money and a non-profit group to exist solely to give money away or help people in need. These generalizations provide for-profit companies with an opportunity to strategically align themselves with organizations that are not seen as profit-driven, thereby lessening the consumer's perception of the for-profit business as being "money hungry." In turn, the consumer becomes more open to hearing a commercial message. Though most cause-related marketing campaigns never send the media or consumers a message of "buy our product/service," a natural result of the collaboration and its resultant media attention is almost always a corresponding increase in sales. The cause-marketing campaign serves as a subliminal message that gives the consumers a reason to feel good about their purchase (and take a break from the incessant commercial messages thrown their way). In addition, the cause-marketing effort gives the for-profit entity a story to tell as an "advocate" for the charity. (The term "advocate" is used herein to describe the corporate partner's role in the cause-marketing partnership, as this can be a primary benefit which it provides to its non-profit partner.)

> **These generalizations provide for-profit companies with an opportunity to strategically align themselves with organizations that are not seen as profit-driven, thereby lessening the consumer's perception of the for-profit business as being "money hungry."**

Let us take a look at how cause marketing can increase sales. As briefly discussed in the introductory chapter, Steve Garrigan of Aspen East Fitness and Well Being Center, a fitness center in Montclair, New Jersey, wanted to boost awareness in the media about his fitness facility in order to increase membership and, in turn, revenues. Partnering with the Spina Bifida Research Resource, a non-profit entity searching for a cure for this disabling birth defect that affects approximately 70,000 Americans, Aspen East, in conjunction with our public relations team, created a media event that generated extensive television and newspaper coverage.

In addition to year-round activities at the fitness center, the team created an annual event in the gym's parking lot whereby members of the public, the Aspen East Cycling Team, and gym-goers peddled spin-cycles for 100 consecutive hours. Because these spin-cycles were in constant motion for 100 hours, as cyclists took turns riding the bikes and raising funds for spina bifida research, several media/photo opportunities were created, and the fitness center enjoyed constant exposure throughout the event. The public relations media alert was headlined "Spin for Spina," and the event resulted in a 30-percent increase in Aspen East's sales.

But the members of media who covered the event did not report a commercial message advertising the gym. Instead, they featured the event as a "feel-good story," applauding the gym owner for raising money for such an important (and little-talked-about) disease. Members, new and old, spoke of the event for months afterward, and the fitness center has replicated the event annually. Because of the photo opportunities available to the press, as well as the different cyclists who provide human-interest stories, the media continue to cover it. (Readers will learn later in this chapter that another outcome of cause-marketing partnerships is that companies enjoy fresh publicity opportunities. Companies which otherwise lack media-centric happenings continue to receive press coverage by participating in cause-marketing partnerships, an upshot that results in an increased bottom line.)

Though Aspen East resolved to raise funds and awareness for the cause, its corporate goals were on top of the mind as well. The gym owner wanted to increase visibility and improve sales. A successful cause-marketing campaign will attract media attention, which translates into a better bottom line. It will also build a company's brand, which means greater awareness of the company and higher sales, particularly because consumers and customers are more interested in conducting business with philanthropically involved corporations than non-charitable-minded corporations.[16] Once again, here was a campaign that improved employee morale, which in turn improved productivity, lowered turnover, and increased profits.

Objective #1: Key Points

The vast majority of businesses want to increase sales or profits. We suggest corporations should include a sales or profit-related objective in their cause-marketing campaign. Objectives that fall under this category might also include:

- *Increasing profit margins*
- *Lowering operating costs*
- *Increasing sales in a specific region*
- *Increasing specific product sales*
- *Increasing repeat customers*
- *Improving productivity*

Objective #2—The Power of Visibility: Cause Marketing as a Tool for Increasing Brand Awareness

Strategists and consultants will tell a company to start considering its exit plan as soon as it opens its doors, even if the owner lacks the intent to sell. This philosophy, shared by business plan-ners across the globe, suggests that by taking the measures that best prepare a company for merger or acquisition, a business owner concurrently takes the same measures that position it for all-around success. Liken this to a homeowner who keeps her house in tip-top shape regardless of whether she is looking to sell it. When she does, the house will command a higher price because it has been well cared for and its systems have been maintained.

Likewise, a business positioned for merger or acquisition is at the top of its game. Appraisers know that a direct correlation exits between a company's brand awareness and its valuation. A well-known company is worth more money, a concept that needs little explanation. Think about this: Without knowing anything about location, ownership, management, staff, or the bottom line, would you rather own a Starbucks or a Java Hut?

Cause-marketing campaigns advance the brand awareness of a company by leveraging media attention and, as we will discuss later, directing media coverage to a company's target audience. Resulting in favorable media coverage that acts as third-party endorsements for the company, cause marketing positively influences the public's perception (whether business-to-business or business-to-consumer) of a corporation or brand's credibility, image, and visibility in the same way that a good public relations campaign does.

Cause marketing helps a business or brand increase name recognition and brand awareness.

Before it partnered with Literacy Volunteers of America (LVA), Famous Amos Cookies had few resources for promoting itself, and the United States' adult illiteracy epidemic was relatively unknown. LVA, which provided tutors for undereducated adults, desperately needed media coverage to educate the public and legislators about the severity of illiteracy and importance of literacy. And Famous Amos wanted to build the company's brand name through grassroots public relations efforts. Though the company lacked an advertising budget, its founder, Wally Amos, did have an outgoing, larger-than-life persona. In a textbook public relations program that is still used as a case study in university marketing classrooms today, the co-founder of our firm, John Rosica, developed a strategic cause-marketing program with Literacy Volunteers of America, which included media events, a national spokesperson tour, and speaking engagements. LVA's purpose in forming this partnership to end adult illiteracy complemented Amos' primary purpose: to brand Famous Amos Cookies and heighten the company's visibility.

Resulting in favorable media coverage that acts as third-party endorsements for the company, cause marketing positively influences the public's perception…

The outcome? Fantastic on all fronts. The partnership generated media placements in *People Magazine*, *A&E Biography*, *Chicago Tribune*, *Today Show*, *Good Morning America*, *The New York Times*, *Time Magazine*, plus thousands of daily and weekly newspapers, food trade publications, and local television stations across North America. The effort spawned national brand awareness of Famous Amos Cookies exceeding 75 percent by 1985. Wally himself received millions of media impressions, which later helped him sell books and succeed in other business ventures.

Though Amos left the business some years prior, in 1998 the Famous Amos brand was sold to Keebler Foods Company, which was later purchased by the Kellogg Company. Today, Famous Amos is a major contributor to Kellogg's $11.77 billion in annual net sales.

The partnership also generated interest in literacy programs and branded LVA across the nation. In fact, the partnership we created was the impetus for then-First Lady Barbara Bush, the most powerful woman on the planet during that time (with the possible exception of Oprah), to develop a personal interest in literacy programs.

Indianapolis 500 racecar driver Mark Smith can testify that selling a business is not the only reason to seek brand-awareness objectives. Before hiring us, Mark Smith was having difficulty obtaining sponsorships. Though he had a primary sponsor—Evergreen International Aviation—Smith needed additional sponsorships to cover the extraordinary cost of auto racing.

Knowing that Smith overcame amblyopia, an eye disorder affecting 2 or 3 percent of people and characterized by poor or blurry vision, we decided to pair him with the Seeing Eye Foundation. Our cause-marketing team invited a blind Seeing Eye Foundation spokesperson and her dog to a media event at the Meadowlands Racetrack at which they both would ride alongside Smith and experience the feeling of being in a race car. Along with four TV crews from New York City and New Jersey and a top daily newspaper, *Parade Magazine* featured Smith on its cover, an honor that no other driver had ever earned. Moreover, Sears Craftsman Tools became interested in Smith and agreed to sponsor him in a multi-year, multi-million dollar deal!

The Seeing Eye Foundation also benefited. Not only did Smith donate a portion of his purse to the cause, but, because of the *Parade Magazine* story, the Seeing Eye Foundation was bequeathed a million dollars by a couple who read the story.

Objective #2: Key Points

If increasing brand awareness is not one of your objectives, you are flying under the radar and very well may crash and burn. Like creating a fresh publicity strategy (Objective #5), goals that fall into this category are particularly important for companies with relatively few new products, which means they have relatively few opportunities to generate news and the public has little opportunity to learn of the company. Unlike some technology companies that constantly release new products (such as Apple), most companies are not able to secure ongoing media attention simply by the nature of the company's products or services. And those that can might be served well by creating a brand that embraces corporate giving.

Microsoft is a perfect example of the power of cause marketing to shift the brand equity of a company. In the late 1990s, the company faced an onslaught of public relations nightmares brought on by anti-trust lawsuits that accused it of unfair competition, predator pricing, and wielding monopoly power. The company's brand was tarnished, but its founder Bill Gates, who was not one to surrender easily, initiated an aggressive charitable-giving agenda. Today, he is considered one of the world's largest philanthropists. Indeed, its good deeds have done good things for Microsoft's brand. Objectives that fall under the category of "increased brand awareness and equity" also include:

- *Increasing a customer base*
- *Attracting media coverage*
- *Building credibility and image*
- *Enhancing reputation and image*
- *Differentiating a brand or company*
- *Strengthening customer loyalty*
- *Positioning the company for a merger or acquisition*

Objective #3—Stopping Clock-Watchers: Cause Marketing as a Tool for Increasing Employee Morale

In a notable survey, 97 percent of employers said the primary audience for their cause-marketing effort was employees.[17] Though their local communities and consumers followed closely, companies recognized that one of the principal benefits of a cause-marketing campaign is an employee base with improved job satisfaction, better overall performance, and stronger customer service.

Other surveys support this. A study of MBA graduates from some of the top American and European schools found that more than 97 percent of graduates said they were willing to sacrifice some amount (on average, 14 percent) of financial compensation in exchange for a company that had a reputation for socially responsible and ethical behavior.[18]

Prior to engaging in a cause-marketing campaign, one of our clients recently reported the following about two of her key employees, both of whom were talented, results-driven, qualified people with proven track records. One, a sales representative, was regularly seen making personal calls and gossiping with other employees. The second, her trusted office manager, took lengthy lunch breaks, indicating that he was either a slow eater or—more likely—extremely unmotivated. Our client was frustrated with her employees' productivity (or lack thereof) and wanted to drive change, for good reason. The statistics about productivity are alarming:

- About 30 percent of workers say they watch sports online while working; 24 percent admit to shopping online during the workday; and more than one-third (37 percent) say they surf the Internet constantly while at work.[19]
- A study indicated that 92 percent of online stock trading

occurs during work hours.[20]

- According to a Gallup Poll, the average employee spends more than 75 minutes daily using office computers for non-work activities. The Department of Labor, Bureau of Labor Statistics, estimates that the average cost of employing an American is $20 per hour; these 75 minutes of lost time translate to a loss of $6,250 per year per employee. Five-employee companies are losing $31,250 to office computer abuse alone; a company with 500 employees is losing $3.125 million per year.

As frustrating as this might be to the employer, and despite the fact that Internet policies are difficult to police, his or her employees are likely even more frustrated. Imagine spending eight to ten hours a day at work, unable to juggle personal life, family issues, bills, and the like. And, frankly, many employees report that their work bores them. Barbara Lament of Canada's national paper, *The Globe and Mail,* approximates that half of the population would answer affirmatively to the following question: *Are you bored with your work?*[21]

With lethargy so prevalent, employees are always breaking the rules and finding ways to make their days personally productive and exciting, despite how busy they *should* be. To be clear, I am not condoning this behavior. But lack of employee productivity always warrants a look at the corporate environment, and cause-marketing campaigns provide an effective tool for addressing demoralized employees.

Cause marketing is an excellent way to improve employee morale.

Quality of work life (morale) is one of the top indicators of an employee's productivity. Those who are more satisfied with their jobs will work harder than those who are dissatisfied with the quality of their work environment. And, of course, employee morale influences other aspects of the work force. Disgruntled employees are more likely to spread office gossip, initiate lawsuits, or create conflict. Workers with low morale will be likely to seek employment opportunities elsewhere, which translates to higher turnover—a costly expense. Many companies consider cause marketing to be an effective tool for bolstering external communications. Though no cause-marketing campaign is complete without publicity, media events, and ongoing promotions, employee involvement is instrumental to a cause-marketing campaign. And by engaging employees in a cause about which they feel passionate, an employer will see a shift in their attitudes; in turn, the entire corporate culture is likely to change.

Employees will appreciate their employers' efforts and find more meaning in their jobs. From experience, we know this united *feeling* results in an employee base that is more productive. Workers will be more likely to spend time on seemingly mundane tasks if they feel that their jobs are worthwhile overall.

Prior to the cause's becoming a nationally recognized non-profit brand, we partnered an engineering and architectural firm with Habitat for Humanity. During summer months, when business slowed for the firm, the company provided a system whereby employees had the option of taking half-day rotations on Friday afternoons to help build affordable housing. This community-relations effort, coupled with our public relations strategies, pointed media attention toward the partnership, which resulted in a proud employee base that became more enthusiastic about civic engagement and the effort and commitment of their employer. A cycle of reciprocity began as employees became more and more involved in the cause, and the media coverage surrounding employees' efforts resulted in heightened morale. The company's image as a productive business member within the community was another tangible change.

According to the company's CFO, "The buzz around the office was spectacular! People were engaged and appreciated top management for wanting to give back and encouraging employees to do the same."

By engaging employees in a cause about which they feel passionate, an employer will see a shift in their attitudes; in turn, the entire corporate culture is likely to change.

Objective #3: Key Points

Regardless of the economy and unemployment rate, heightened employee morale should be a goal of most companies, especially those fighting to attract or retain the most talented workers. Cause marketing is a brilliant strategic component of a competitive benefits package, and we encourage all readers to include this objective in order to hire and retain the best talent.

Indicators that you should consider improved employee morale when determining your cause-marketing objectives include:

- *Low employee productivity*
- *A gossipy/work-force clique*
- *Disgruntled employees/former employees*
- *Difficulty finding the right employees*
- *A hostile working environment*
- *Workers who complain that they are not fairly compensated*
- *A substandard benefits package*
- *Low employee pride*
- *High turnover*

Objective #4—Fighting Fires: Cause Marketing as a Tool for Preventing or Managing Crises

Though linguists across the globe debate its authenticity, the story goes like this: The Chinese character for the word "crisis" (translated from the ideogram to *wei ji*) is a merging of two ideograms. One Chinese ideogram represents the word "opportunity" (*ji huay*); the other symbolizes "danger" (*wei xian*).[22]

Regardless of the story's legitimacy, it offers a lesson served by self-helpers, therapists, and motivational speakers. A crisis is the convergence of danger *and* opportunity. Will you face the danger so that you can seize the opportunity? Or will you succumb to the fear, miss the opportunity, and look weak or guilty?

For a company threatened with a crisis, opportunity can come in the form of a cause-marketing campaign, which is the best form of public relations for a corporation suffering from the threat of negative publicity or the experience of bad press. Offering more than just "spin," empty words, evasion, or a combative and defensive attitude, cause marketing attacks the crisis, beats it down, and helps a business come out on top. By helping our clients communicate their good news, many clients in the midst of a crisis emerge on the other side as victors, stronger than before, with a solid image intact.

To be clear, we do not recommend being reactive but rather proactive with cause-related marketing. In my firm's thirty years' experience counseling hundreds of clients in their cause-marketing endeavors, we have gathered much empirical evidence indicating that a company that proactively and regularly disseminates its positive attributes and news will more readily overcome crises or any blemish when and if a crisis hits. Therefore, we recommend ongoing positive awareness to quell potentially negative stories that could hurt business.

Offering more than just "spin," empty words, evasion, or a combative and defensive attitude, cause marketing attacks the crisis, beats it down, and helps a business come out on top.

This brings us to the next of the top five objectives most companies have when developing a cause-related marketing campaign.

Cause marketing quells the fires of a crisis (and circumvents future crises).

As stated previously, we suggest that a company engage in a cause-marketing campaign proactively, before the crisis hits. In ideal circumstances, a business would implement its campaign to build awareness, employee morale, and respect in the community and among consumers or business partners. But short of this, the company should initiate the campaign at the first inkling of trouble.

A company suffering from a publicity disaster has a mountainous challenge. Not only must it overcome the stigma already associated with corporate America, but it also must counter, block, and avoid a quarry of rocks being thrown its way. After taking a beating, the fastest way for a company to emerge in a positive light is to enlist the help of the media through a strategic cause-related marketing effort that encourages the target audiences to embrace or at least appreciate its good work. By garnering positive media coverage, the public (and media) can forget, or at least forgive, past discretions.

Consider African Pride, a hair- and skin-care product line that targeted the African-American community. Our client, the Caucasian owner of African Pride, was suing a black-owned company for trademark infringement over the name African Pride.

Revlon's African Pride Brand partners with Birthing Project USA.

At first, the dispute was merely a matter of trademark protection, but when a consortium of African-American hair companies learned that an African-American-owned company was being sued by a white-owned company over the name, they waged a campaign against the owner, distributing negative publicity to the African-American community and called for a ban of African Pride products. The community activist Reverend Al Sharpton sent boycott letters claiming that African Pride was not a friend of the African-American community to such retailers as Kmart and Wal-Mart. These sanctions could have buried the company.

Never before had the company faced such a potentially threatening quandary. It was in danger of losing support from the target demographic which its products served. Fortunately, African Pride's founder immediately hired us to help manage the crisis.

We connected African Pride with Birthing Project USA, a non-profit organization dedicated to improving the lives of pregnant minority mothers with newborns. At that time, Birthing Project USA was a struggling agency. It was also the perfect match for African

Pride because it already had strong ties to the African-American community and addressed infant mortality, an emotionally charged subject affecting this population at a disproportionate rate.

At the first media event held by African Pride and Birthing Project USA, the company's CEO was photographed holding babies helped by the cause and his corporation's involvement. He also donated $100,000 to the non-profit entity to prevent it from folding. Over a seven-year period, the company enjoyed literally billions of positive media impressions. As the organization grew, the CEO knew he had succeeded in portraying his company in an accurate and positive light.

Soon after kicking off the campaign, we sent Reverend Sharpton a white paper that told the story of Birthing Project USA, as well as African Pride's involvement. He was left with no choice but to abandon the boycott. African Pride was a friend of the community, and in years to come the company donated dollars, visibility, and numerous employee volunteer hours to the cause. How could Sharpton possibly convince the community that African Pride was anything other than a friend of the black community?

By circumventing this crisis, African Pride emerged stronger than ever, with sales that consistently beat the industry average. The company's brand equity skyrocketed as a result of the partnership, and Birthing Project USA gained considerable awareness. As well, its chapters grew by 25 percent within the first three years of the partnership. A few years later, Revlon bought African Pride because of its strong ties to African-American communities, which were forged through the aforementioned efforts.

In retrospect, African Pride's founder said, "I never thought this crisis would present an opportunity to grow our brand equity, image, and ties to the African-American community. We wanted to do the right thing, so we took our new public-relation firm's counsel, and it more than paid off."

Particularly important to quelling a crisis is a company's ability to dominate the first two or three pages of online search engine results. If your organization is paired with a cause, Google's algorithm will respond favorably by placing your organization higher in search results, and by awarding your organization with a notably higher page ranking. By taking proactive measures to concurrently manage your online reputation, news of a crisis within your organization might be secondary to the good will you enjoy by virtue of your relationship with a cause.

Objective #4: Key Points

We suggest that all companies embrace this objective, regardless of whether the company has a crisis on the horizon. Planning ahead to avert crises is easier (and more effective) than waiting until one hits, at which time many companies begin scrambling to salvage their image and livelihood.

If your company is facing a crisis, particularly if it is in the form of negative media, this goal should be at the top of your list. Otherwise, it will be a natural outcome of any effective cause-marketing effort. Objectives that fall under this category might include:

- *Countering the effects of a lawsuit*
- *Redeeming a company's brand equity following a crisis*
- *Responding to a publicized executive scandal*
- *Creating a strong relationship with the media*
- *Strengthening your brand and enhancing your reputation*

Objective #5—Time for a New Story!

How does a company sustain visibility and keep itself in the spotlight in the absence of new product or service offerings and announcements? The challenge of creating constant buzz so that a story can continue to emerge through online and traditional media is particularly demanding on those companies that do not constantly generate new news (which is a talent any good public relations firm should constantly be uncovering). Many companies fall to the wayside, engulfed by newer, hipper competitors who offer updated products with flashier logos and trendier attributes or ingredients. Failure to maintain publicity and word-of-mouth can be just as damaging as negative media coverage, and it can be the death of a company. Therefore, we offer cause marketing as a key strategy to keep you in the headlines, on the Web and on television and radio newscasts.

Though the media might have been interested in a company's story when it first opened its doors, the business will quickly become yesterday's news unless it devises a strategy to keep the story fresh. So how does a company overcome this obstacle?

Cause marketing is a method of creating a fresh publicity strategy with ongoing media coverage.

Through a cause-marketing campaign, a business can continue to secure media coverage even when little else is happening within the organization. By joining forces with a non-profit entity, a company can create a unique opportunity and timely reason for telling its story through proactive media relations.

When Stew Leonard's, then an emerging Connecticut dairy farm and retail store, asked us for help in creating buzz, we immediately saw an opportunity. When you think "dairy farm", you do not think "exciting", yet the effort we embarked upon caught fire.

Stew Leonard's needed to create a fresh publicity strategy and strengthen its ties to the community. Our solution was a community-focused cause-marketing campaign whereby we installed a wishing well where customers could donate change to a charity. Weekly, Stew Leonard's matched the donations to the wishing well, and donated the offering to a different local charity. This created an ongoing media-friendly photo opportunity and publicity!

In this case study, Stew Leonard's reached out to 30 or 40 local charities.[23] In doing so, it met its objectives of strengthening its ties to the community and created a novel publicity strategy. After we ended our relationship with Stew Leonard's, the strategy lived on and, despite a major crisis, the dairy chain bounced back and has continued its growth (which also demonstrates the crisis-fighting power of cause-related marketing).

Despite the crisis and bad press, remember that Stew Leonard's made its way onto *Fortune* magazine's "Top 100 Companies to Work For" that very year. Today, the dairy chain does nearly $300 million in annual sales with 2,000 employees.

Objective #5: Key Points

Would you like to secure ongoing media coverage? Does your company need to strengthen its community ties? Re-emerge regularly in the public's eye? Improve its online presence?

For most companies, newsworthy events are hard to come by. Cause marketing helps disseminate fresh, timely, relevant, and newsworthy stories to help the company secure ongoing media attention. If your business is not creating ongoing news opportunities and generating media coverage on its own merits (with a solid public relations strategy), include this objective in your cause-marketing goals. Remember, too, that Microsoft continues to engage in cause-related marketing even though it constantly introduces new products. This helps prevent crises and softens the corporate giant's image by demonstrating compassion. A solid corporate citizen is hard to criticize or dislike.

The Objective-Setting Process

As much as possible, *The Business of Cause Marketing* mimics the process we take with our clients when developing their cause-marketing campaigns. First, we ask a series of questions that help us elicit our clients' business objectives. Note that this process seeks information about their *business* objectives, not just their marketing or philanthropic objectives. These include short-, intermediate-, and long-term goals. While we also like to discuss marketing goals, the process is first and foremost concerned with the business from a macro perspective. The reason is twofold. First, a company often fails to realize the ways in which a business aspiration might be met by a cause-marketing strategy. For instance, companies might not consider cause marketing as a method of retaining employees. Second, identifying business objectives will help better determine what direction to take the cause marketing effort in. A business-to-business company that needs to ramp up international sales has different marketing priorities from a company that wants to appeal to consumers or to a particular community. The former is less likely to adopt a cause-marketing platform; however, we have found cause-related marketing to be extremely effective in business-to-business marketing, particularly for those looking to improve customer loyalty or employee morale, or in highly competitive environments and in cases where margins are limited. Here's why:

- Everyone in society—including business owners, key decision-makers, and executives—has a consumer mindset. We are all consumers, and consumers prefer to do business with cause-involved companies. As such, business partners, existing and prospective, respond favorably to those who are not just "in it for themselves."

- Employees respond favorably to this practice, and your customers might benefit from their involvement.
- Because you have a higher purpose, price will not be the only factor in your prospective customers' decision-making process.
- Joint volunteer efforts with business-to-business affiliates can garner mutually positive media coverage and buzz within the trade. This can also boost tradeshow marketing efforts.

If you are moving forward without the guidance of a cause-marketing strategist or are executing the effort utilizing your senior marketing staff, I strongly recommend that you address the following questions in a collaborative setting, drawing on feedback from key executives and/or employees. Because this is a discovery process that refrains from assigning right or wrong answers, your objectives will be strengthened and enhanced by incorporating as much feedback as possible. If you are the CEO or chief marketing officer, I urge you to solicit feedback and then follow your instincts. In other words, do not make the final determination by trying to please everyone. After all, as the company's owner or CEO, you should know the company and its marketing and image needs better than anyone.

Questions to discuss include:

- Looking at your business plan and objectives, what will your company look like in one, three, five, and ten years? How do you want people to think of you? What are your business challenges? How could awareness and cause marketing benefit your bottom line?

- What reasonable growth can you expect to see under your current marketing plan?
- How has the economy affected your short- and long-term business goals? What would a five- to seven-percent increase in re-orders or customer retention mean to your bottom line?
- What one word or phrase would your clients use to define your company?
- What is your brand? What phrase, category, solution, feeling, or issue do you own? Or, for what feeling, brand promise, or point of differentiation do you want to be known?
- What is your 30-second elevator speech?
- What differentiates you from your competitors? (I suggest spending time considering this and finding the essence of your company rather than simply defining your products' or services' features and benefits, because finding the essential differentiation speaks to your brand image and how people will relate to your company.)
- Would your clients call your company philanthropic?
- Is employee retention a top priority? What does it cost you to hire, train, and replace staff-level employees? Managers?
- How would you describe your average employee's workday or week? Stressful? Competitive? Demanding? (Refer to the survey in Step Five for a measuring tool to gauge employee perception.)
- What are the stressors or negative feelings that your employees face while at work?
- How would your employees describe their workday or week?
- What would they say about the company atmosphere?

- Is your turnover rate acceptable? How much money would you save annually if you were able to retain employees on average an additional twelve months? Eighteen months?
- How strong is your company's ability to sustain a promotional agenda?
- Do the media express constant interest in your company? Are the media overwhelmingly positive? Are you regularly featured and not just mentioned?
- Does the nature of your business provide an ongoing flood of online and traditional positive media exposure?
- If your business does provide ample publicity opportunities, how would charitable involvement enhance your image and positioning?
- Would your company survive a scandal? What's at risk?
- Do you have a crisis plan in place?
- What legacy do you want to leave behind?
- How can cause marketing help you reach your objectives?

Upon receiving feedback and engaging in this discovery process, you should have enough information to solidify your key messages and objectives. When crafting objectives, keep in mind that goals should be SMART: Specific, Measurable, Attainable, Relevant, and Time-sensitive. Pages 66 through 68 discuss this concept in more detail.

Put your objectives in writing. You will need to refer to them as we move through the process of developing a cause-marketing campaign. Creating written goals turns abstract concepts into concrete, tangible forces. Legend tells the story of the researchers who in 1953 surveyed Yale University's graduating class to determine how many of them had written specific goals for the future.

Twenty years later, researchers polled the same members of the class and found that the 3 percent who had written goals in 1953 had amassed more personal financial wealth than the other 93 percent of the class combined. That this urban legend is a myth does not negate the power of written goals. Motivational speakers, business coaches, and consultants around the world have empirical evidence that companies as well as individuals are more likely to achieve their goals if they write them down.

We also suggest posting your goals in a place visible to all employees and managers involved in implementing the campaign. In *The Strangest Secret*, Earl Nightingale revealed his secret: "We become what we think about."

Scientist, philosopher, and author Emmet Fox said, "You think, and your thoughts materialize as experience, and thus it is…"

A simple corollary of this is: You get what you focus on. By posting your objectives and vision, you will have a constant reminder of your goals and you will engage your team, which means you will be more likely to achieve success.

* * * * * * * * *

SMART Goals

Most business owners have at least heard of SMART goals. SMART isn't a proprietary or novel concept, but it does work. SMART goals are **S**pecific, **M**easurable, **A**ttainable, **R**ealistic, and **T**ime-sensitive, and they help a company pinpoint exactly what its goals are. Setting SMART goals also allows a company to create a gauge by which it will measure a cause-marketing campaign's success. By creating goals that are SMART, companies have quantifiable means of assessing outcomes.

Within the SMART paradigm, **Specific** means that the goal is detailed and precise. "To grow my business," is vague. It fails to define the parameters and list specifically what the business owner wants. How many new clients are we striving to acquire? Do we need to build any systems to accommodate this growth? If so, which ones? If repeat business or retention is a priority, what is our specific target percentage? What is our net profit percentage goal? How often do we want to reach out to prospective customers and how many should we focus on? How many media events will we have to ensure ongoing awareness? Here are examples of specific goals:

- To employ 250 people
- To acquire 10,000 new customers
- To increase recurring orders by 18 percent
- To retain 100 percent of "A" players
- To garner 50 million "free" media impressions
- To granularly measure the impact of our marketing efforts (trade show, public relations, advertising, Internet, e-mail, and the like) as related to sales.

Measurable goals are those that are quantifiable. Because the goals above were specific, they are also measurable. They set criteria for measuring the success of a goal and usually involve a number, ratio, percent, or dollar amount. As discussed in detail in Step Five, most objectives are, in fact, measurable, even those such as employee morale and customer perception of a company, both of which can be determined by surveys.

Attainable simply means that your goal is possible. If your last's year's net profit was $3 million and you normally enjoy a 13 percent per annum growth, is it likely that you can quadruple your profit in one year? If you are a five-person company, can you realistically increase staff to 250 within the year? Within three years? SMART goals are those that can be accomplished. We like setting aggressive goals, but remember to set your company up for success rather than for failure. Stretch the rubber band—don't break it!

Realistic goals are those that are appropriate for a given team or company. If your employees are responsible for implementing your cause-marketing campaign, make sure they understand the objectives. If your goal is "to increase the profit margin by 4 percent by end of year," be sure that all team members understand how a profit margin is calculated, including the factors (cost of goods sold, markup, overhead, and profit) that ultimately drive the bottom line. If employees do not feel connected to the goal, they will not be as ready to leverage those activities that will help the company reach its intended outcome.

Time-sensitive goals. Determining a clear time frame will help keep you on track and will allow you to recognize the stepping stones necessary to reach your ultimate goals. Have your management team assign deliverable dates to establish expectations and increase the likelihood of your cause-marketing campaign's success.

The following goals address all elements of the SMART formula (assuming they are relevant to your business and attainable by your company):

- To increase net profit by $7.3 million in the third quarter as compared with Q2
- To lower employee turnover to 5 percent by year-end (particularly when unemployment is low)
- To garner 50 million media impressions quarterly

It's More Than Just the Money

While determining your own objectives is paramount in creating a cause-marketing campaign, understanding your non-profit partner's objectives is critical to the eventual outcomes of the effort. Though few non-profit entities turn down donations from corporate sponsors, it bears noting that corporations engaging in effective cause-marketing relationships understand that their cause partner's objectives extend beyond donor solicitations. As we discuss further in subsequent chapters, non-profit organizations generally want one or more of the following from their cause partners:

- **Increased awareness.** If this is not a primary goal of a company's non-profit partner, the partnership might be in trouble. Most, if not all, true cause-marketing partnerships are intended to generate media awareness. (From our experience, this is the key to goal achievement. How else can you tell your story, reach your customers, and help the charity?) A cause partner, such as a runaway shelter, which avoids media attention, will jeopardize the objectives of a corporation looking for increased sales, a fresh publicity strategy, or heightened brand awareness. As such, the best cause partners are hungry for media attention, which is why the term "marketing" does appear in cause-related marketing but does not appear in its cousin, corporate social responsibility.

- **Increased volunteerism.** Though increased volunteerism is usually an outcome of increased awareness, a cause partner might need immediate assistance from people in the business community (your people). A cause partnership is complementary when the corporation wants to boost employee morale and its non-profit partner wants to increase volunteerism. By lending its employees to a non-profit entity for a few hours each week, a corporation will immediately see heightened morale as its employees begin viewing their jobs as being worthwhile and meaningful.
- **Access to business resources.** Non-profit entities do not have the resources of talent that are available to for-profit businesses. It is entirely common to see a non-profit entity directed by employees who have a solid understanding of the non-profit group's mission but often lack the strategies necessary to achieving these missions. A corporation engaging in a cause-marketing partnership can increase its own employee morale and, at the same time, impart its business know-how for the benefit of the cause partner by allocating employees with skills, knowledge, or resources to its non-profit partner.
- **Resource development.** Let us not forget that a non-profit group's budget is financed entirely by its donors. A cause-marketing relationship is symbiotic when the corporate partner can donate money, resources, or goods to its non-profit partner and, in return, increase brand awareness, avoid crises, build sales, or create a fresh publicity strategy.

- **Legislative support.** If you have strong ties with local, state, or federal policymakers, or if you have a strong lobbying firm representing you that can benefit your cause partner, this can go far to solidify the relationship and add value. Your charity partner will go the extra mile to cross-promote the relationship, and this will pay dividends.

A cause-marketing partnership is most rewarding when the objectives of the non-profit and the for-profit groups are in sync. By determining up front what you wish to acquire from the campaign and what your likely cause partner will expect, you will be more likely to find the best possible cause and engage in a profitable marketing partnership that achieves mutually defined goals.

Chapter 3:

Conducting a Cause-Marketing Audit & Choosing a Cause Partner

A cause-marketing audit represents the confluence of a company's "pure motive" and its "profit motive." A company's pure motive is its emotional reason for choosing a specific cause. The pure motive considers the philanthropic interests of the company's employees, managers and, most importantly, its CEO, founders, or principals. It is driven by passion, humanitarianism, and the desire to positively impact a community. The pure motive can be the heartfelt story behind the partnership, lending authenticity to the campaign and thereby separating it from the purely tactical (and overly transparent) corporate-non-profit partnerships that consumers know exist in order for the corporate partner to look good. The pure motive is the company's answer to the following question: Why this cause?

A profit motive, on the other hand, considers whether partnering with a specific cause will be feasible, realistic, and effective at accomplishing the company's objectives. The profit motive is the strategic and tactical mission separating corporate philanthropy (charity for the sake of charity) from cause-marketing (charity as a deliberate and calculated business decision, which can considerably help the company and the cause) and philosophical ideology to drive business while positively influencing the corporate culture and the world.

A cause-marketing audit represents the confluence of a company's "pure motive" and its "profit motive."

While a company's pure motive is significant, especially insofar as the CEO genuinely embraces it, the profit motive drives the program, defines its goals, and provides a standard by which success can be calculated. If the cause-marketing partnership realizes positive outcomes, all parties—shareholders, consumers, CEOs, and the cause—come out on top. While at first glance this seems to be more evidence of corporate self-interest and "greed," cause marketing has a positive impact on society and employees alike—it allows the consumer to embrace not only the cause-marketing agenda but also its corporate advocate. Doing good not only helps a company do well and realize its goals, but it also promotes the cause and inspires others to join forces in making a difference, as previously discussed.

While a cause-marketing campaign is shaped by a company's profit motive—a strategy intended to reach a company's business, marketing, and sales goals—it is this success that enables it to thrive and give more. A smart cause-related marketing agenda achieves its goals and, by its mere endurance, continues to positively impact the world or a community. In other words, though the profit motive is the partnership's engine, its very existence allows the pure motive to survive. Upon failing to achieve its profit objectives, the heartfelt objectives of an improperly executed cause-marketing campaign are thrown out as well.

As instrumental as the profit motive is, much attention should be paid to a company's pure motives before it selects a charity to advocate. The ideal charity is one in which the collaborative effort with the non-profit entity not only increases the company's likelihood of reaching its objectives (profit motive) but also allows employees, managers, and stakeholders to participate in a cause about which they feel passionately (pure motive). If the CEO, founder(s), or principal of the for-profit company lacks a genuine and personal connection to the cause or an interest in bringing attention to it, they might as well give the partnership the kiss of death. Their profit motives will be transparent and, instead of masking the commercial message, the cause-marketing partnership will accentuate it, causing consumers and customers to question their motives.

An exploration of a company's pure motive is particularly crucial when the CEO and other executives are not partial to a particular charity. By tapping into employee resources, a corporation can use its people to discover charitable options that may have been initially unclear. That being said, the cause with which some employees most connect might not be the optimal one.

Most companies get cause marketing all wrong. They either have purely selfish motives or do not disseminate their philanthropic efforts often enough. As you can see, the ultimate cause partner selected is based on a mixture of micro- and macro-variables. In considering each of these factors, we start with a genuine concern with helping others.

Examining the Pure Motive

Vital to the success of a cause-marketing campaign is its ability to communicate an authentic motive that the public (or target audiences) can embrace. As such, developing a strong campaign requires a company to provisionally abandon words such as *strategy*, *intention*, or *objective*. The for-profit partner should (temporarily) concern itself

Most companies get cause marketing all wrong. They either have purely selfish motives or do not disseminate their philanthropic efforts often enough.

with discovering its passion. What issues tug at the company's collective heartstrings? Remember that the company's heart is comprised of top executives, middle management, and line employees. All three ideally will unite and concurrently embrace and support the cause. As a cause-related marketing campaign stimulates media coverage, the company's principals will often advocate the charity and speak on behalf of the partnership during media interviews. If these leaders are not enthusiastic and supportive of the charity or issue, the media and the ensuing public will view the partnership as insincere or staged. In *The Authentic Brand*, I discuss the importance of a company's ability to create a unique brand that engenders the feeling of authenticity. Thanks to the effortless availability of information, today's buyers are savvier than ever, and companies must respond to their knowledgeable consumers with honest, legitimate, and smart brands. Consumers have become more educated and, in turn, more skeptical about sales tactics. They are inundated with competitive offerings and vendor marketing messages—consequently, there is a need to stand apart as a company that reveres integrity.

As we discussed earlier, a critical advantage of cause marketing is its ability to de-commercialize a commercial message. Yet, it must recognize and reconcile the quandary created therein. Though the cause-marketing partnership is a profit-driven strategy, its co-existing mission must be to propel a genuine motive and advocate a cause. If cause marketing is done year-round and a company commits to regularly advocate for the charity, the campaign demonstrates the company's good intentions. A company's heart has to be in it.

Keep in mind that the cause-marketing partnership must embrace the pure motive that it is using to advance its profit interests.

Consider the partnership between Wishbone Salad Dressing and Make-a-Wish Foundation. Without a doubt, this partnership was borne of strategy, intention, and objectives, and the public knows it. Wishbone Salad Dressing seems to have hinged its entire campaign on the commonality of the word "wish", which certainly might please a poet, but comes across to the general public as disingenuous—even if it is not. Perception is, after all, reality. And though Make-a-Wish Foundation is a worthy cause, and Wishbone Salad Dressing is an equally worthy advocate, the duo's partnership seems contrived entirely of Wishbone's profit motive. Given today's general distrust of U.S. corporations, coupled with the availability of blogs and websites dedicated to exposing corporate greed, the public is often deafeningly critical of or quietly cynical about such partnerships, which give skeptical consumers one more reason to consider switching to competitive, more down-to-earth brands.

Case Study: Gary Hirshberg and Stonyfield Farm

Led by entrepreneur and philanthropist Gary Hirshberg, Stonyfield Farm is a shining example of the power of companies that produce authentic, down-to-earth brands. Stonyfield Farm is surely at an apparent marketing disadvantage. Its marketing budget is a mere fraction of that of its competition, yet the New Hampshire-based innovator sent Yoplait, Dannon, Breyers, and other top players in the yogurt and dairy industry scratching their heads in wonder because of its successful and unique grassroots marketing approach.

As reported in The Authentic Brand, *Stonyfield's innovative approach was to infuse a smart "geo-branding" campaign leveraging its New Hampshire farming roots with a cause-marketing effort. Before we can examine the brilliance of its marketing campaign, let's take a quick detour to define geo-branding.*

Geo-branding, a phrase coined by Rosica Strategic Public Relations, is the concept of marketing a company so that its brand is associated with a specific geographical location. This is yet another tool companies often use to turn their corporate image into a "down-home" feeling. Samuel Adams used Boston, Coors is synonymous with Colorado, Starbucks with Seattle, Ben & Jerry's with Vermont, and Burt's Bees and Tom's of Maine with Maine. Though the consumer products offered by Samuel Adams, Coors, Starbucks, Ben & Jerry's, Burt's Bees, and Tom's of Maine are hungrily consumed well outside their respective boundaries, their geo-branding efforts have created a personal, anti-corporation feeling that bonds their consumers to a perceived friendly way of life. Though many are now part of giant conglomerations, these corporations seem almost rustic, and therein lies their charm. Vermont, for instance, conjures up a clean, pure, simple, and natural feeling. Colorado is associated with mountain water and the rugged outdoors, and Seattle with rainy days that beg for a cup of hot coffee. With their provincial, country-store branding, organizations that apply geo-branding tactics often create an authentic and trustworthy brand.

Stonyfield Farm concurrently branded itself as a community store and "local" dairy farm, rejecting the corporate feel of big businesses. In latching onto the cornerstone feeling, Stonyfield Farm told its consumers that it was averse to greed, impersonalized service, and corporate waste. Indeed, its unsophisticated packaging supported this brand, telling consumers that Stonyfield Farm was more interested in good quality than superficial flash or appearance. The company's geo-branding efforts complemented its community relations and cause-marketing activities, and Stonyfield integrated environmental programs in all marketing efforts. The company created the Lid Program, a consumer-education initiative whereby each six-ounce lid used on a Stonyfield Farm product is printed with educational information that provides consumers with key health and environmental facts. As well, the company donates 10 percent of its proceeds each year to projects that protect or restore the earth, primarily those that are based in New Hampshire. (A lengthy interview with Hirshberg, who coined himself company CE-Yo, can be found in The Authentic Brand.*)*

Hirshberg's success and business practices are innovative in their ability to create real value, making the company worth more because it maintains genuine concern for our planet. Due to Stonyfield's unique identity, positioning, and resultant appeal, the company has taken hold of a significant piece of the yogurt industry and is now selling other dairy products, including milk, with tremendous success. The company's pure motives have resonated with all who have experienced the brand, even Stonyfield's competitors, many of whom have adopted Hirshberg's ideas and decided to advocate non-profit groups of their own. Further pointing to the company's brand equity, since 2001 the Danone Group (Dannon's parent company) has acquired 85 percent of Stonyfield's shares.

Companies whose executives do not completely embrace and become emotionally invested in the success of the advocated cause will appear to have ulterior motives and will be received as if they do. Executives lacking the pure motive might also be accused of hiding transgressions.

This disingenuous attempt at cause marketing is especially apparent during the holiday season. From mid-November through the New Year, countless mega-corporations bestow food, toys, or a percentage of their proceeds to worthy causes, primarily centered around impoverished children and their destitute families. Their charitable giving stops (or appears to) as soon as the holidays end and the crowds dissipate. Today's savvy consumer, probably correctly, interprets these minimal attempts at philanthropy as marketing ploys driven by advertising.

On the other hand, if top management genuinely supports a cause-marketing campaign and creates a year-round program that incorporates charitable giving *and* charitable involvement, the company's sincerity will be reflected in the media's attention and the consumer's approval. When Wally "Famous" Amos followed our suggestion and joined in league with Literacy Volunteers of America, Amos invested his heart and soul in the cause. A high school dropout, Wally's aunt imparted to him the magnitude of opportunities offered to educated Americans. (Incidentally, Wally's aunt also cultivated his love of cookies.) It was, in part, this lesson that allowed Amos to realize such success as a businessperson. After hearing Wally's story, the media responded favorably, and the public soon followed. Despite all of the opportunities afforded to Amos through the partnership, the public knew that Wally supported the cause wholeheartedly. Wally's relationship with LVA had nothing to do with the dollars he donated; instead, he brought awareness to an important issue. People everywhere, as well as the media, knew he meant what he said about the role which reading played in his life and about his sincere resolve to fight illiteracy. The crux of Wally's campaign was not the dollars that were donated, but rather the awareness brought to an issue. This heightened public sensitivity is the lifeblood of any corporate campaign.

Rallying the Troops

Unlike key management, an employee's support (or lack thereof) for a cause partnership likely has no bearing on the media or the public's response to the campaign. However, having employees engaged and involved will help morale, which has a resultant positive effect on the company's image and bottom line.

Consider Whole Foods, the country's largest natural and organic supermarket. As discussed in the introductory chapter, Whole Foods is an avid supporter of local causes, engaging in several cause-marketing efforts. It also pays its employees to donate time to community and service organizations. Not coincidentally, the company has won a spot on *Fortune* magazine's annual list of the "100 Best Companies to Work For" each year since the list began nine years ago. The largest factor influencing this list is a survey that asks randomly selected employees to answer questions about job satisfaction, camaraderie, and attitudes toward management.

Based on the results of the survey, it is safe to assume that Whole Foods has strong employee morale.

Without question, this community involvement helps Whole Foods attract and retain a higher quality employee. While we are uncertain what the future will bring, with the majority of food retailers now shelving and promoting organic and natural foods, not surprisingly, the company also enjoys an average sales growth of 5.4 percent.[24]

Starbucks is another example of a corporation that has realized the corollary between employee satisfaction and cause-related activities. Though many of its line employees lack college degrees, Starbucks offers a competitive benefits package that includes comprehensive health care, a stock-option plan, a stock-investment plan and a 401(k) plan. It also supports its employees' charitable contributions by matching up to $1,000 annually per employee. While at work, its employees participate in community-service activities. During the holiday season, the company organizes a toy and book drive for children suffering from serious illnesses. Like Whole Foods, Starbucks has been on *FORTUNE*'s list of the "100 Best Companies to Work For" a mind-boggling seven times. Its latest employee satisfaction survey shows that 87 percent of its employees are satisfied or very satisfied at work (as opposed to only about half of mainstream America's employees). And 73 percent of Starbucks' employees feel engaged with their job—extraordinary results for a corporation that primarily employs non-skilled workers who have little room for lateral growth.

How are all these factors related? It is not without coincidence that a company's pure motives are often in line with its profit motives. Without a doubt, if employees are happy, a company will have a better chance of achieving its goals.

Ask Gordon Bethune, former CEO of Continental Airlines.

In the five years following Bethune's 1994 inauguration as CEO of Continental Airlines, the stock rose about 17,000 percent and the company reported 12 consecutive quarters of record results. Prior to his term, Continental Airline's flights were on time only 61 percent of the time, a staggering 18 percent below the industry's average. Moreover, everyone hated the airline, including its employees, travelers, and shareholders.

Then Bethune was hired. Under Bethune's decade-long direction, the company started winning award after award. For seven years in a row, it was named as one of *FORTUNE* magazine's list of "100 Best Companies to Work For." It won "Airline of the Year" from Air Transport World and "Best Airline in the U.S." The accolades just kept coming. Despite its prior poor record of on-time flights, the company won "No. 1 On-Time Performance" from the U.S. Department of Transportation, "No. 1 in Customer Satisfaction" from Frequent Flyer/J.D. Power & Associates, "No. 1 in Customer Service" from SmartMoney Customer Service Awards, and "No. 1 in Customer Loyalty" from Brand Keys Survey.

Why the sudden change? Bethune cited a "100-percent correlation between customer satisfaction and employee satisfaction" and created strategies for improving the quality of work life at Continental Airlines.[25,26] His "Go-Forward" plan to combat the issues at the airline included a heavy component that resolved to improve employee morale. The employees responded, as did the company's profits. In large part due to his focus on employee morale, Bethune was credited with saving Continental Airlines from extinction.

Certainly, a company can improve employee satisfaction through bonuses, benefits, and various morale-booster strategies.

Bethune's program included profit-sharing and performance-based bonuses, as well as a reward program whereby employees with impeccable attendance were entered in a drawing to win a new car. Other companies with smaller budgets attempted to boost morale by instigating "Casual Fridays" and "Hawaiian Shirt Days," etc.

These methods have varying degrees of success, yet nothing changes the corporate culture faster and more positively than engaging employees in a cause-marketing campaign. A recent survey found that 56 percent of corporate marketers with cause programs noted heightened employee morale and retention as a key benefit.[27] By soliciting input from employees, and then using this input to direct a cause partnership, a company will notice that employees have better attitudes, as well as enhanced productivity, and they are more likely to speak positively about their workdays, thereby enhancing productivity, and, in times of economic growth, recruitment efforts. Employees find themselves excited to come to work. They swell with pride as their companies are featured on nightly newscasts or websites or national (or regional) magazines, and they enthusiastically plow through their daily activities, knowing that they can donate free time to the cause-partnership activities. Both the cause and the employee benefit. The company enjoys greater sales, offsetting time which employees might devote to the cause instead of to their day-to-day duties.

But a company cannot expect its employees to support just any cause. Unlike key management and ownership, most employees (even those whose wages are low or are commission-based) will be uninspired by a cause-marketing campaign about which the CEO is not passionate. Employees are often influenced by pure motive. Therefore, walking the walk is critical, as is having everyone in the organization aware, involved, and informed.

To kick off a cause audit, we ask our corporate clients to ascertain those causes about which their employees are passionate. As we discussed earlier, we are particularly concerned with feedback from the CEO, yet we ask our clients to consider the opinions of every employee, including key executives and entry-level employees, especially if employee morale is an issue. Do not leave anyone out. If your mail clerk is sick or on vacation, make a mental note to ask for feedback when he or she returns. Remember that the pure motive reflects the heart of the company, its collective emotions. An overlooked employee will feel as if his opinions do not matter, creating a situation that is counterproductive. Retaining part-time and entry-level employees might not be high on a company's list of priorities, but remember that the college student in your mailroom might become your next sales manager. And any company with employees knows that employees, especially disgruntled ones, talk—a lot.

Conduct your cause audit in person—either individually or in groups—rather than by e-mail or memo. One reason for auditing your employees is to help your workers see that their opinions count. E-mails and office memos are impersonal, and they fail to communicate that sentiment. If the cause relationship is important enough to warrant a meeting, your employees will see that you are serious and genuine about the efforts.

When soliciting feedback, we suggest that a company's CEO bridge any disconnect between management and employee by leading the cause audit. Obviously, this becomes more challenging in a 50,000-person company, in which case a CEO should first solicit feedback from key management/executives, who can then meet with "employee feedback teams" or conduct "town hall meetings" defined by geography or department.

Nothing changes the corporate culture faster and more positively than engaging employees in a cause-marketing campaign.

Regardless of the format in which you solicit feedback, a company should ask the following questions of each employee, including its owners or principals (but, depending on how closely held the stock, not necessarily shareholders of publicly traded companies):

- Which organizations have you volunteered for? Donated to?
- Which charities/causes pique your interest? Why?
- Are there any specific causes that have impacted you or your family?
- Do you sit on the board of any non-profit group?
- What philanthropic activities would you like to engage in but don't have time for?
- Are there any causes you are adamantly opposed to?
- If the company were to "adopt" a charity, which one should it be and why?

This should be a brainstorm session, and keeping it simple will help its facilitation. Do not engage employees in a lengthy debate about which causes might or might not work. Though your employees' opinions are valuable, from experience, we recommend controlling the process. Listen to their suggestions and take notes. If you are soliciting feedback in a group setting, allow your employees to feed off each other's ideas, but do not allow an environment in which employees are critiquing each other's suggestions. Each employee should walk out of the meeting feeling as though his/her voice will be fully considered.

In concert with the cause audit, begin rallying your troops. Tell your employees why you are engaging in the cause-related marketing campaign and what it will mean for them, your customers, your affiliates, and the community at large. Give them written information about the cause. If applicable, specifically communicate that the campaign will allow them to donate work time to a charity of their choice which they can support (if you can commit to this), or tell them of the partnership and what it will mean for recipients of the non-profit entity and how the company will help. Your employees want to know that their time at work has relevance and their company is making a difference. Expanding their job description to include advocating a cause can also help your employees feel more purposeful about their jobs, which then drastically alters their perception of the corporation.

As we discuss in detail during Step Five, upon assessing employees' interests, most of our clients report an immediate shift in employees' attitudes, as well as productivity.

What Does a "Pure Motive" Look Like?

In short, a pure motive offers a personal connection between the cause and the for-profit company advocating the cause, with the operative word being *personal.* As I mentioned earlier, the pure motive answers the following question: *Why **this** cause?* A corporate CEO, principal, or founder should be able to answer this question with a personal story, whether it be his/her own, a family member's story, or an employee's story. The best partnerships stem from an affiliation between the owner, the founder, or a CEO who keeps the efforts alive.

Racecar driver Mark Smith's pure motive for supporting the Seeing Eye Foundation was his personal experience with an eye condition. One of our clients, a small retailer, supported a job-preparedness program because one of her key employees, an immigrant who at first struggled with the language, had been hired through this program. Her story offered an emotional tie to the cause, highlighting the authentic reason behind the partnership and helping the company achieve its profit motive.

"It's a good cause" is *not* an answer that offers a personal connection.

A genuine story illustrating a CEO's connection to a charity or a fight against a social ill creates an authentic emotion that can spawn a powerful and memorable cause-marketing program. The story must be real and told through media events, traditional PR, Internet PR, and social media.

Examining the Profit Motive

Despite the profit-driven objectives of a cause-marketing campaign, executives often find themselves pulled toward a cause-marketing partnership that is driven entirely by *pure* motives. They like the idea behind a certain non-profit organization, and they want to make the partnership work. Yet the top priority of a cause-marketing partnership is to meet the company's marketing and profit-driven objectives. If such are achieved, the program will be self-sustaining and make a greater impact. Although individual or corporate support can be given to any charity, many otherwise worthy charities do not make ideal cause-marketing partners, and they must be set aside to make room for a cause partner that will help the company meet its profit goals.

Many executives report discomfort when asked to examine their company's profit motives and temporarily disengage from their emotions. "I kept coming back to the same thought:

These charitable causes ***matter***," said one of our clients, a health care-products manufacturer.

We addressed this by pointing out a few things. According to the National Center for Charitable Statistics, nearly 1.4 million non-profit organizations exist in the United States alone. Even if only 10 percent of these organizations represent a worthy cause, we still have 140,000 causes from which to choose. Therefore, we must use *some* criteria to narrow the list of causes to which we donate time, efforts, and dollars. And, in a cause-marketing campaign, a company generally must pick one primary cause or risk its effectiveness. Why not narrow down the list by picking a *good* cause or a debilitating social ill that will also help the company do *well*?

Expanding their job description to include advocating a cause can also help your employees feel more purposeful about their jobs, which then drastically alters their perception of the corporation.

Though we suggest that a company should limit the number of causes with which it aligns to one partner or general theme, we also remind our clients that a cause partnership is between a *company* and a non-profit group. It does not preclude *individual* executives, employees, principals, or stakeholders from donating to other charities. We encourage employees and principals to volunteer and engage with the company's cause partner while still promoting volunteerism and charitable involvement in as many causes he/she chooses.

ROSICA
Online+Traditional Public Relations & Marketing

95 Rt. 17 South, Suite 202
Paramus, NJ 07652-3700
Tel: (201) 843.5600 Fax: (201) 843-5680
www.rosica.com

--MEMO--

A meager 5 percent of charitable dollars are raised by corporations, and these dollars are spread among the 1.4 million charities in America, as well as countless charities abroad. Yet non-profits groups run almost entirely on donor support. Many lack not only the donations but also lack volunteers to implement their worthy missions.

What if we could make a difference with an important charity? How many lives could we affect? And how would it feel for all of us, together, to give back?

We are about to find out! Join us today for a mandatory meeting: We want your input in choosing a charity partner!

Time: 3:00 p.m. – 4:00 p.m.
Location: Conference Room 2

ATTENDANCE IS REQUIRED! YOUR FEEDBACK IS CRITICAL!

Can a Company Partner with Multiple Causes?

A strategic cause-related marketing program generates a strategic partnership between a corporation and a single non-profit group (or theme). The marketing campaign should have focus and engender recognition and widespread awareness, making the commitment and involvement known and appreciated. However, a cause-marketing partnership does not preclude an individual employee, executive, or stakeholder from donating or volunteering to other charities on his/her own time. Rosica's team includes individuals who serve on boards for various charities, including United Way, Eva's Village, Project Literacy U.S., Salvation Army, Boys & Girls Clubs, Hispanic Chamber of Commerce, Gilda's Club, and others. We encourage this personal involvement, while at the same time having one literacy organization which we support as a company.

Finally, we remind our clients that we will never ask them to abandon their pure motives. Instead, we ask that a company temporarily set aside its pure motive and consider its business and marketing objectives. After identifying the profit motive, the company can search for a cause that fulfills the pure motives and is able to fulfill the strategic goals.

With that out of the way, we are free to move forward examining the criteria used to determine the causes that might address a company's profit motive. It bears noting that we make no judgment as to the merit of a non-profit entity's mission, nor do we offer our opinion on non-profit groups' administrative efficiencies. Indeed, our executives support a variety of non-profit groups with varying levels of sophistication, some with world-renowned missions and others with limited operations and service areas.

As strategists, however, we must determine whether a cause partner will work and whether it will effectively help our for-profit client achieve its goals. Indicators that a non-profit group will *not* make a good cause partner include:

- The cause does not want media attention.
- The community served by the non-profit organization cannot be exposed to the media or general public or wishes to be "under the radar."

- The bureaucratic nature of the non-profit entity limits its flexibility and hinders progress.
- The non-profit group's extreme political or social position might compromise a company's neutrality.
- The non-profit organization has already enjoyed tremendous recognition and media attention.
- The non-profit entity is too conservative or restrictive.
- The organization does not need you.

Keep in mind that these criteria have nothing to do with the overall worthiness of a cause and instead simply dictate whether the cause would make a good marketing partner. Therefore, causes that rate high on the profit-motive scale will:

1. Be hungry for awareness and demonstrate a thirst for heightened visibility.
2. Offer their constituency, time, and commitment to the media relations and marketing partnership's efforts.
3. Maintain an open mind and take counsel from their cause-marketing partner.
4. Provide good visuals or "pictures."
5. Be neutral rather than extremist in their socio-political views.
6. Be "up-and-comers."
7. Resist logic and be open to creativity.

Let's consider each criterion.

A Hunger for Awareness

Your cause partnership is, in large part, about building a strategy for securing ongoing media attention. Therefore, finding a cause that is yearning for media attention is critical to achieving your marketing objectives.

Yet be aware that, central to their mission, certain non-profit entities must protect the community they serve from media attention. Such partners will not support your media-centric goals. One of our clients is passionate about helping women who have been abused. The owner sits on the board of a battered women's home where she has been volunteering for over a decade. Her commitment and passion are unquestionable, yet the shelter would not be the best cause for her company or for any corporate partner. Inherent in the name "shelter" is the idea that these homes assist abused women who must, of necessity, seek privacy in their search for a safe haven. Such facilities protect their typically transient residents from their abusers; therefore, any media attention would be counterproductive and probably harmful for obvious reasons. Such homes, however worthy in nature, do not make good corporate cause-marketing partners. Instead of media attention, they need donations of clothing, toiletries, kitchen accessories, and dollars. They also need discreet volunteers and mentors, pro bono legal counsel, grief counselors, job-preparation liaisons, and the like.

As individuals or as corporations wishing to make private donations, our clients should donate their personal resources (time, resources, skills, etc.) to such causes; as corporations seeking cause partners and media attention, they should not. At a minimum, the corporation will be limited in its ability to publicize the partnership. More likely, it will be forbidden entirely from disclosing any details about the partnership to the media, taking the "marketing" out of cause marketing. As you can see, visibility is vital in a true cause-marketing campaign.

Non-profit groups that support overwhelmingly debilitating illnesses might also be inappropriate, since many of their community members will not feel dignified in having the effects of their diseases publicized. (We'll discuss later that these causes often create stark and depressing images.) Again, let me reiterate that personal involvement in these non-profit groups is desperately needed. Media attention, however, is not only unwarranted, but, in many cases, also unwanted.

Instead, find a charity that wants online and traditional media attention as much as you do. If, for any reason, the cause is interested in donations and not brand awareness, it may not appreciate or embrace efforts to garner awareness.

A refusal to engage in media campaigns most often happens when the charity is limited due to the community members it serves. Other organizations, already enjoying a high profile, are simply uninterested. We discuss this later in the section titled "Up-and-Comers."

* * * * * * * * * *

A Note about Foundations

Many of our corporate clients who create charitable foundations want to fly under the radar, fearful that they will be bombarded with non-profit groups seeking charitable contributions. Attracting media attention is the dominating purpose of a cause-marketing campaign; do not be reserved when soliciting media attention Instead, simply create a formal application program that weeds out solicitations from non-profit entities whose missions are not germane to your organization. Some smart foundations do engage in proactive promotions and marketing activities. This helps them achieve their organizational goals more effectively.

If you do not desire media coverage, cause marketing is not appropriate for you. Instead, consider the foundation approach.

Offering Constituencies, Time, and Commitment

Part of the inherent difficulty of a non-profit entity is its lack of financial and human resources. For these reasons, non-profit groups are not expected to contribute dollars or resources that cost money (such as marketing materials) to a cause-marketing campaign. The cause partner is not, however, a charity case and can and should contribute its constituencies, time, and commitment to the cause-marketing campaign.

Herein, we use the term "constituencies" to describe the community served by a non-profit group. Like finding a charity that is media-hungry (and often for the same reasons), a corporation's profit motives are best served by those non-profit groups that will provide easy access to their communities. Central to a cause-marketing effort is the availability of photo opportunities and events that demand media attention. Certainly an organization dedicated to helping children in need is worthy, yet if the organization is unwilling to allow its minor constituents to be filmed, you will have a problem executing media-friendly events, even if the non-profit group is otherwise in favor.

You might also use the constituent base to help build awareness for an event. Imagine creating a media event whereby a mass of people is needed for a photo opportunity. Who better to participate in this public relations activity than those served by the non-profit group? Also look for an organization that is able, willing, and eager to share the results of the partnership with the media.

An equally important consideration is the non-profit group's willingness to avail itself to the partnership. During a media campaign, partners will often need to make quick decisions and be immediately accessible for interviews and press opportunities. If the non-profit organization's director or leading executive does not make this a priority, ensuring time and a committed effort, find another partner.

* * * * * * * * *

Taking Counsel

As an advocate of its cause partner, a company's role in a cause-marketing partnership includes providing counsel to its non-profit partner. Unlike non-profit entities, which are generally run and staffed by people invested in fulfillment of the cause's mission, for-profit companies typically have a diversified work force with a variety of skill sets. In this scenario, the corporation houses the skills and business acumen necessary to propel a company forward.

This is not to say that the cause is less capable. Rather, the cause is understandably focused on implementing a mission, helping its constituents, and bringing critical aid to the needy. Non-profit groups often lack the time, energy, and resources necessary for long-term strategic planning and effective communications.

While this lack of equivalent business acumen seems problematic in a symbiotic relationship, the contrary is true. Heeding the advice of its for-profit business partner allows the non-profit organization to create two opportunities. First, it is able to grow from the business skills imparted by the non-profit group. Second, it removes the "too many cooks in the kitchen" syndrome from the formula, which then makes for a smooth partnership.

* * * * * * * * * * *

Providing Good Pictures

Considering that one primary goal of a strategic cause-marketing campaign is securing media attention and that the media effectively uses pictures to tell stories to our increasingly graphic or visual society, a partnership which addresses a company's profit motives should be completely media-friendly. The best way to ensure mass-media coverage that includes magazines, social media, daily newspapers, television, online news, and radio is to paint a compelling, interesting, or one-of-a-kind photo opportunity (picture). Or, use YouTube to post good images on your website each week. Either way, we say: Create good pictures and the media will come.

Centuries ago, mainstream America revered the written and printed word, but today's stories are image-driven, with the quality of the written word taking the back seat to sensational images. Our abbreviated 21st-century attention span causes the media to rely primarily on compelling pictures.

A shining example of the importance of pictures is illustrated in the 1989 savings and loan crisis. Paul Muolo, executive editor of *National Mortgage News*, noted that "most of the media missed the S&L crisis."[28] Why? A former top national network television executive explained that the media did not cover the S&L crisis, the biggest news in decades, because "there were no pictures to tell the story."

This gets to the heart of what can make or break a media event, photo opportunity, news conference, interview, or any publicity effort. We need good visuals that will attract the media and help tell the story. If the media ignored the biggest news in decades because that story failed to produce engaging visuals, imagine how the media will respond to your corporation's soft-news story if it is not accompanied by friendly images.

If the cause-marketing campaign is properly developed and executed, with strong pictures as an attention-getter, the media will respond. If covered by the print media, without question the best possible exposure a cause-marketing partnership or any public relations initiative can hope for is a photograph and caption clearly identifying the company. With the flood of images we receive on a daily basis in our contemporary society, particularly on the Web, a picture will catch people's attention faster than an article. When gauging the success of a campaign, we prefer a photograph and caption to a 300-word article without an associated image. Needless to say, we strive for both the copy *and* the all-important photo, but images are more important than words any day of the week. My father always says, "If a picture used to be worth a thousand words, in contemporary society its value has been inflated to three thousand."

Whether the coverage is broadcast or print (or preferably both), the media will want it to be visually appealing. My public relations agency began using the term "saturation marketing" in the early 1980s to best describe the effect a grassroots public relations effort has within a demographic marketing area. This local-market media blitz, which is executed concurrently with a national media campaign, is likened to the dropping of a pebble in calm water. The rings spread in concentric circles similar to the mental ripples of awareness caused by the public relations effort.

This type of media coverage optimally will be in the form of feature stories. Newscasters and journalists reporting these stories are not in search of a fair and balanced, hard-hitting, objective item. They want good news and heartwarming images, something to balance the bad news that fills newspapers and airwaves. They want to broadcast or publish content and images that make their audiences feel good, and they rely on public relations people, corporate or agency, to help them source their stories. The frightening or depressing images simply will not suffice without some positive, inspirational, and emotionally stimulating news and pictures. With the power of social media, including photo and video sharing and social networking, these images help connect with people and can generate viral word-of-mouth communication successes.

Strong photo images have the added advantage of persuading the media to take immediate notice of a story. Generally, feature stories are not time-sensitive and can be pushed to make room for other high-priority news events. Creating compelling photo opportunities works to provide incentive for the media to cover the story with immediacy. Without a strong image, media outlets might not feel compelled to cover the piece, regardless of its merits.

When considering your cause-partner options, remember to ask yourself: *Can we paint a good picture in conjunction with the cause partner and its affiliates?* If you cannot think of a creative strategy

"If a picture used to be worth a thousand words, in contemporary society its value has been inflated to three thousand."

to fashion an upbeat image for the print, broadcast, and online media, consider discussing this with a media or public relations strategist before moving on to another cause. Media-relations specialists can create a compelling image out of the seemingly mundane, so beware of abandoning otherwise-great causes without first brainstorming for events that would allow for media success. If your company feels strongly about a cause supporting children with chronic skin issues, you might not fare well if your media event is held in a hospital filled with sullen children. However, if your media-event scenario, which you plan to roll out in cities across the country, places these children outside to witness a hot-air balloon inflation and learn the science of hot-air ballooning, as we did for a balloon-festival promoter who needed our help, you will fashion a strong, friendly image and, in turn, create an opportunity to support both your cause and your company at the same time.

In the same cadre as "creating positive pictures" is "creating strong pictures." If you cannot think of a single image (happy or otherwise) that would accompany media events held in collaboration with a specific cause, consider another partner—or hire someone adept at creating strong images.

Neutral Causes

Unless your clients are exclusively conservative Republicans, you probably do not want to consider a Christian cause. Likewise, we suggest steering clear of controversial organizations such as

Planned Parenthood, which has a tab on its website's navigation bar calling for visitors to "take political action."

Because your client base is likely diverse, aligning yourself with religious or political affiliations will exclude a large segment of your target market. And if your goal is to increase your bottom line, this makes for poor strategizing.

Instead, choose causes that the majority of the population can support. Many organizations are obviously exclusive. We are all aware that pro-choice issues will invoke a strong emotional response. We know that aligning with Catholic-affiliated causes might exclude our Jewish, Islamic, Protestant, and Mormon clients. Consider, though, that some organizations are not easily recognizable as religious/political entities. Habitat for Humanity is best known throughout the nation as a charitable organization that builds homes for homeless people throughout the world. However, one visit to its website lets us know that the organization is an "ecumenical Christian housing ministry." That said, Habitat for Humanity does not position itself as religious to its corporate partners or to the media.

And how about animal organizations? Supporting the local humane society might seem like a good idea. Surely, it will paint some pretty pictures, but consider the political ramifications. Does the humane society euthanize its animals? If so, it is probably only slightly more criticized than the "no-kill" shelters, which are sometimes condemned for leaving animals in cages for years without putting an end to their suffering. And let's not forget PETA. As perhaps the largest and most recognized animal-rights organization in the world, People for the Ethical Treatment of Animals is regularly in the news, but rarely is the news positive. It is either defending its actions or attacking a makeup line, clothing company, or household product. Given the split over animal rights and the strong emotions involved, use discretion when selecting charities focused on helping animals.

We recently looked to pair a corporation with the Southeastern Guide Dog's program, Paws for Patriots™, which provides seeing-eye dogs for men and women of our armed services who come back from combat blind. Though the cause is quasi-political in that it serves the military, the organization is dedicated to helping people—war veterans—and sentiment regarding such a charity is almost entirely inclusive. This is not to imply that the company or the cause supports the war—it may or may not. One thing is for certain: It supports injured soldiers coming home.

Poor Images	**Strong Images**
A ribbon-cutting ceremony	A chain-cutting ceremony with bolt cutters outside a local library with a caption that reads: "Cutting the bonds of illiteracy"
A ground-breaking ceremony	Fourth graders in hard hats with giant shovels breaking ground
An oversized check for $10,000 presented to a non-profit entity	The world's smallest $10,000 check presented along with a magnifying glass 12 inches in diameter
A press conference to acknowledge the corporate partner of a cause campaign	A 12-foot tall "thank you" card presented to the company for its commitment and contributions with all in attendance signing the card in support of the cause
A company placing an ad or uploading information about supporting a cause that lowers infant-mortality rates	A cause-marketing media event with dozens of moms holding their babies impacted by the cause partnership—surrounding the corporate partner's CEO who has volunteered and donated to make it all happen

Up-and-Comers

Common sense dictates that the bigger the cause partner, the better the outcome. Similar to landing a large client, corporations often believe that partnering with a mammoth cause is the key to success. Hasn't everyone heard of the American Lung Association? Doesn't Susan G. Komen have more resources, longer donor lists, and already established media ties?

Yes, yes, and yes.

So why do we advise *against* cause partnerships with well-established charities? The primary reason is that these charities do not *need* to partner with you. They are already branded and have companies competing to support them; therefore, they are less likely to be accommodating. They already have the spotlight; they already have massive resources, lengthy donor lists, prestigious boards, and media exposure. Against conventional wisdom, we tell our clients to partner with smaller, lesser-known causes that are *up-and-comers.*

Need to create a "mediagenic" image? Kick off any cause-marketing partnership with an old-fashioned true-to-life "kick off."

This advice might go against your instincts, which tell you that the bigger the cause, the better the opportunity. As you are about to learn, up-and-comers provide fresh news and are highly likely to attract the media. At the same time, their for-profit partner's message is not lost. Smaller, focused, and hungry charities will embrace their corporate partners because they know this relationship will help them become mainstream and/or achieve their goals.

Let's consider Alisa Unger Designs, a jewelry designer who wanted to join forces with a giant breast-cancer research foundation by donating a line of jewelry to the non-profit entity. Alisa was surprised to learn that the $1 million donation she offered over three years was not enough! Unless she could guarantee millions in donations a year, the Susan G. Komen Breast Cancer Foundation refused to allow her to advocate the charity and declined to pursue the relationship. This non-profit group, run exclusively by donor dollars, refused to engage in the free national public relations campaign which the company offered to execute on its behalf as a cause advocate. The jewelry designer had an authentic story and reason for approaching this charity: She had two family members who died from breast cancer. This particular non-profit entity, like most well-known charities, is so popular that it is supported by major car manufacturers, makeup companies, and sporting good stores. Though I am certain it helps people who are suffering, it is able to cherry-pick its corporate partners and demand an extremely high price (for instance, a guaranteed yearly contribution amount) to advocate it.

Assume, for the sake of argument, that you *are* able to secure a partnership with a nationally known non-profit entity. Even if a giant does want to partner with you, the benefits are less than ideal. For one thing, mammoth non-profit organizations are typically in search of dollars—*big* dollars. Large non-profit groups have their own staff and plenty of volunteers. They have budgets for media campaigns and their own brand awareness. They have relationships with partners that often sponsor national co-branded ad campaigns. They likely have celebrities championing their causes. These giants cast a big shadow, and you could get lost in it. Moreover, if you bring attention to a cause which you are advocating that is relatively unknown but affects many throughout the nation or world, you will bring attention to yourself.

The Susan G. Komen Breast Cancer Foundation is arguably one of the best-known non-profit organizations in the world. A charity that has spread national awareness about breast cancer, the Komen Foundation is supported by a list of impressive donors: BMW, Hallmark, Lean Cuisine, Ford, Yoplait, and Bank of America are just a few of the 172 corporate sponsors listed on its website. To date, BMW has raised over $13 million for the Komen Foundation; Yoplait has donated more than $20 million; and Ford has given more than $100 million in financial and in-kind donations since 1995.

This year, McNeil Nutritionals, LLC, is donating $100,000 to the charity, and Mohawk Industries has pledged a minimum donation of at least $250,000. But who cares? Compared to Yoplait, BMW, and Ford, McNeil Nutritionals and Mohawk Industries seem like small players. The stakes are high, and if the players do not keep up, they will be lost in the shadow of the Komen Foundation and its massive supporters.

Moreover, though breast cancer research is a worthy cause, it has commanded the spotlight for the better part of 20 years. It may garner media coverage with a barrage of stories during Breast Cancer Awareness Month, but the news media are unlikely to consider that breast-cancer awareness stories are new, instead opting to use them as "filler" on a slow news day. Many corporate "partners" get lost in the mix, and their efforts are not genuinely valued.

Former First Lady Betty Ford, upon surviving breast cancer, first brought this disease to the forefront in the mid-1980s with an emotional televised appeal for breast-cancer awareness. Since then, the appeal has decorated October with pink ribbons for nearly two decades. During National Breast Cancer Awareness Month, a long list of major organizations—including Playtex, Cartier, Estee Lauder, *Mamma Mia!* and Coach—have hosted "pink-ribbon" events, supporting activities that raise awareness for breast cancer, a cause that has become synonymous with a pink ribbon.[29] Though a worthy cause, the slew of companies that have jumped on board with pink-ribbon campaigns make it challenging for corporations to separate themselves from the pack (though not impossible, as you will learn from our "Light Up the Night in Pink" case study on page 151).

National Breast Cancer Awareness Month has become so popular that a non-profit organization (Breast Cancer Action) has created a campaign, "Think Before You Pink," to educate consumers about which companies to support—and which to avoid—during National Breast Cancer Awareness Month. Breast Cancer Action calls breast cancer "the poster child for corporate cause-related marketing," warning consumers of companies that are trying "to boost their image and their profits by connecting themselves to a good cause." Though "Think Before You Pink" does not provide specific counsel on which organizations to support and which to avoid, it certainly makes its objections known.

After commenting on a car manufacturer's donations to a breast-cancer foundation, the "Think Before You Pink" website notes that "components of car exhaust...have been linked to breast cancer..."

Describing a dairy product that donates to the same foundation, the same website writes that "many cows are given rBGH... Recent studies show that rBGH dairy products may be linked with an increased risk of breast, colon, and prostate cancer."

A sure sign that a non-profit entity is too big to serve as your corporate partner? When another non-profit or advocacy group launches a campaign against its cause-marketing efforts!

Nationally known giants also threaten to stall your cause-marketing campaign with cumbersome guidelines. Such organizations might restrict your ability to advocate them in creative ways, hindering liaisons with the media by dissecting your press materials and website copy or limiting the type of media exposure you garner. While often these behemoth charities are not in any way pliable, due to increased competition among local non-profit groups, we have occasionally found local chapters of national charities to be collaborative, strong cause-marketing partners. But before joining forces with such an organization, ask them the following questions:

- How would you rank your top marketing and organizational priorities and objectives?
- On a scale of one to ten, how would you rank the goal of increased visibility?
- Do you have a public relations agency? Is this a pro-bono relationship? If not, do you handle public relations internally? How would you rate your current public relations results?
- As layering our joint message is vital, how willing are you to execute joint public relations events?
- Would your director make himself/herself available for interviews and media events?

- Is your CEO's schedule flexible enough to accommodate the often last-minute and urgent deadlines of the media?
- In a cause partnership, are you looking for monetary support only? Are you interested in unconventional and creative methods of support, such as employee volunteers, in-kind products and services, or media relations support?
- What is your process for reviewing press materials and how quickly can we get approvals?

If the non-profit entity is already a household name, it may be too big to serve the needs of a productive cause-marketing campaign. Instead, look for an up-and-coming cause-marketing partner. Search online for non-profit organizations that are generating a stir in the media, but are still relatively unknown.

* * * * * * * * *

Causes That Resist Logic

Robert Frost perhaps said it best: "Two roads diverged in a wood, and I—I took the one less traveled by, and that has made all the difference."

In other words, think unconventionally. There are always exceptions to this rule, but before you break the rule, read on.

What if I told you that our client, a specialty veterinary clinic, joined forces with an animal-rescue shelter in a cause-marketing campaign? Do you want to know how and why the partnership was forged, or is it obvious? You can probably tell simply from the nature of the two organizations that their missions are aligned, that they share a common goal. Your interest or the media's interest in the partnership likely ends there. Most likely, you have few, if any, questions. Your curiosity has not been piqued.

But what if I told you that the veterinary clinic partnered with a non-profit group that provides resources to children with autism? Have I piqued your interest now? You might have a few questions. *Why is a veterinary clinic involved with autistic children? What is the connection? Why this partner? What's the story?*

Upon asking questions, you learn that the owner of the veterinary clinic has a niece afflicted with autism. The veterinarian is interested in helping researchers involved in animal therapy, a cutting-edge experimental treatment whereby autistic children are paired with "canine companions." You learn that, in early trials, autistic children have shown increased social interaction and communication when in the presence of animals. The veterinarian and his staff members are helping the non-profit group to coordinate play dates, whereby researchers will observe the interaction between trained canine companions and autistic children in a relaxed setting.

After learning about the partnership, you find yourself emotionally invested in the veterinary clinic. You think to yourself: *This is the kind of veterinarian I want caring for my pets.*

Without even realizing it, you have been sold a commercial message by a for-profit corporation in business to make money. Nonetheless, you are inspired by the pure motive of the partnership, and you wanted to hear more about the veterinarian because the story was authentic and real, because it wasn't formulaic.

On the other hand, the partnership between the veterinary office and the animal-rescue shelter was predictable and not engaging. It lacked an emotional hook that allowed you to feel a genuine connection to the veterinarian. It seemed contrived, and this is something to avoid if you wish to create a valid and strategic cause-marketing program.

We caution against logical partnerships primarily because they are all too common and so they make for uninteresting stories. They do not demand further inquiry or interest, nor do they appear to be genuine, which is a word you will hear over and over again when learning about the proper way to engage in cause-marketing campaigns. Contrary to common sense, a good cause partnership often seems nonsensical, begging you to ask: *Why this partnership?* How many food manufacturers are aligned with food pantries? Perhaps tens of thousands! While nothing is more important than feeding the hungry, whatever the number, the partnership is old news and most of the time not enough to generate media buzz and inspire others to lend a hand.

Conversely, if a partnership tells a good story (with a good picture), the media will jump at the opportunity to give their readers or viewers a feel-good story about a corporation that is giving back in a unique way. People will take notice.

Aside from its inability to spark interest, a logical partnership has another pitfall: It often appears too disingenuous. Though your cause-marketing campaign should always be driven by a profit motive, the partnership should not be obviously intended to increase your earnings. If you partner with a logical cause and try to promote your company as a corporate philanthropist, your constituents will hear your commercial message loud and clear, and your campaign could backfire with the public's accusations that you have selfish instead of selfless motives. Cause marketing is not a forum for a blatant commercial message.

But if your partnership is original, if you have a good picture and public relations personnel who know how to hone and "sell" the story to the media and to your constituents, you can and will succeed. Customers will applaud you for "giving back," and, at the same time, your corporation will effectively disseminate its commercial message while doing good in the community or for those in need.

To be sure, we should explain our admittedly loose use of the word "logical." *We are not* counseling you to throw reason to the wind and follow your heart. We want you to keep your business agenda and choose a partner that makes sense. We do not, however, want your partnership to be obvious and dull. Instead, opt for a creative partnership for your external communications program that does not seem contrived.

* * * * * * * * *

The Pure-Profit Paradox

Examining each potential non-profit cause with these criteria in mind keeps a corporation focused on its objectives. Because we believe that most consumers are driven by pure motives, by good will rather than by strategy, we continue to emphasize that a company should always place more weight on its profit motive than its pure motive when considering its ultimate cause-marketing partner. However, based on a company's objectives, the so-called "pure motive" is often in the company's best financial interests.

Let us consider two companies. Alpha Company has strong sales, its brand equity is high, and its customers are loyal. Its profit-to-revenue ratio, however, is out of whack. The company's overhead is too high, in part because the aggressive sales staff experiences a high rate of burnout, which brings annual turnover to nearly 30 percent. Though Alpha Company, like any company, would never turn down an increase in sales, its primary objective is to reduce expenses associated with training new staff by lowering employee turnover 15 percent by year's end. Finding talented employees is costly and is a major challenge for the company because its workers must have highly specialized backgrounds.

On employee-satisfaction surveys, workers at Beta Company, on the other hand, routinely give high marks to questions about the company's quality of work life. Beta Company has low employee turnover and high morale among its workers. Like Alpha Company, Beta Company also has an unfavorable profit-to-revenue ratio, but for another reason: Its sales have been impacted because its competitors have lowered their prices in response to a downshift in the economy. As a result, Beta Company's foremost objective is to increase sales by 20 percent within six months of implementing the cause-related marketing campaign.

Alpha Company's workers, who often feel overwhelmed and underappreciated, need a morale boost. By listening to its employees and implementing a cause-marketing campaign driven largely by pure motives, Alpha Company can expect to improve the quality of work life and achieve lower turnover rate. (It is not coincidental that the company's profit motives will also be addressed by higher employee morale.)

Unlike Alpha Company, because Beta Company's employees already have high morale, the company can be more concerned with overall sales and less focused on the emotional well-being of its typically happy and engaged employees. But make no mistake about it, Alpha Company, which chooses to place more emphasis on its employees' motives (pure motives), and Beta Company, which stresses the bottom line (profit motive) over employee morale, are both following their profit motives.

The deciding factor here is the company's original objectives.

> **We strongly suggest that you select only one partner as your cause-marketing collaborator.**

If the company does not prioritize a boost in employee morale, place less emphasis on its employees' wishes than on the strategic, mediagenic tactics determined by its executive marketing staff or cause-marketing counsel, then those objectives must be altered.

Choosing One Primary Cause Partner

Ultimately, corporate principals should select the cause partner. Though we strongly suggest that employees be audited, top management is primarily concerned with the profit interests of the company and its image, while employees are concerned with the pure motives. Therefore, the top executive is best suited to eventually select potential partners that address the objectives of the business.

At the end of a cause audit, a company will likely have identified several potential cause partners that can both satisfy its profit motive and be embraced by top executives, middle management, and employees. We strongly recommend that you select only one partner as your cause-marketing collaborator. A successful cause-marketing effort is a partnership, which implies two equal entities. Though it might seem wise to engage in as many causes as possible, our experience has shown otherwise. We have found that companies that align themselves with too many causes are less likely to achieve recognition, awareness, improved customer loyalty, and cause-association than those who "own" just one.

By engaging in a cause-marketing effort with more than one charity, companies look unfocused. They appear to jump on the opportunistic bandwagon and do not effectively disseminate their good news and charitable affiliations. Just as having too many bosses means that an employee essentially has no boss, too many partnerships mean that the corporation will not be recognized for its link to a cause partner.

And, multiple partnerships can look insincere—as though the company is throwing around charitable dollars in an effort to appeal to as many consumers as possible. Trying to be all things to all people dilutes your message and makes media relations lackluster at best. This is not to say your business model does not warrant smaller-scale support of multiple causes; however, engaging in such support does not equate to a strategic cause-marketing program—nor should it replace one.

Keep it simple. Remember to choose one cause-marketing category or partner with the following characteristics:

- Media-"hungry"
- Willing to offer its constituents
- Open to counsel
- Media-friendly in terms of images
- Neutral
- Up-and-coming
- Illogical
- Supported by key management and, most importantly, the CEO

We occasionally counsel our clients to own a singular category rather than a singular charity (childhood obesity, literacy, the environment, or the like). We helped Stew Leonard's erect a wishing well in its dairy store, the proceeds of which were donated to a variety of local causes supporting the *community*. Stew Leonard's campaign worked because the idea was innovative. No other company had used a wishing well so cleverly, and the partnership supported the company's desire to position itself as a friendly, neighborhood store. Stonyfield Farm has many cause partners, yet it has created a reputation as an avid supporter of a variety of healthy and environmentally-friendly initiatives. The cause which Stonyfield "owns" is Mother Earth. For the most part, however, staying focused and layering the message to tell the story typically requires selecting just one primary cause partner, as stated earlier.

By now, you are likely to have at least one potential cause partner in mind. The next chapter will help you determine whether a specific collaboration will benefit both parties and enable both the for-profit and the non-profit groups to identify mutual goals and solidify the action plan, defining expectations and meeting objectives.

Chapter 4:

Establishing The Cause Partnership

While the prior chapter focused on selecting a cause partner with your company's profit motive in mind, this chapter focuses on establishing the partnership and clearly *defining* all roles and responsibilities. Most cause-marketing partnerships make the mistake of defining their relationship as one based solely on the financial bestowments of the for-profit partner. Such relationships ignore the symbiotic nature of a cause partnership; also, in their haste to establish the relationship, they ignore the unconventional, strategic contributions that each can donate to the partnership.

The Non-Profit Mindset

Before a corporation can establish the value-added benefit which it can bestow upon the cause it advocates, it should first appraise the non-profit entity's mindset underpinning its needs. A cultural divide between for-profit and non-profit groups traditionally leaves them speaking two different languages. While corporations are usually driven by profit motives, fundraising goals and missions drive non-profit groups. Despite the fact that non-profit groups must raise dollars in order to survive and accomplish their objectives, those involved in this work tend to lead with their hearts and often lack the infrastructure and business resources (people, systems, planning) to best actualize their missions. Men or women who have been personally affected by a disease or disability or have suffered societal impoverishment often found non-profit groups. These driven and passionate individuals have been inspired to change the world (or a particular community), and their expertise is in addressing a social ailment, not necessarily in devising strategy. Corporations, on the other hand, are usually founded by businesspeople inspired to run a business and earn money. They likely have been educated in business lingo, and they are therefore skilled in accounting, human resources, management, sales development, and marketing—or they have assembled a qualified team to make up for any shortcomings. In other words, while a for-profit entity is driven by profit motives, a non-profit group is generally driven by pure motives; while a for-profit group leads with its head, a non-profit entity usually leads with its heart. Though the non-profit group must stay afloat, especially in light of increased numbers of charities competing for philanthropic dollars, media attention, and volunteers, it most likely focuses on surviving rather than on thriving. This is good news for both partners: It means they have much to offer each other.

What You Give

When approaching a non-profit partner, a corporation should first consider what the cause's precise challenges and opportunities are. Sure, the non-profit partner is looking to raise dollars, and a for-profit corporation can help achieve this in several tactical ways. Given the vast number of charities that exist today, these groups are competing for donors as much as corporations are competing for clients. Not only are we being bombarded by for-profit groups' commercial messages, but we also have a myriad of charities soliciting donations each year. Providing corporate dollars to help fund a non-profit entity is imperative, yet the partnership should not focus exclusively on dollars. After all, the non-profit group's goals likely extend far beyond its fiscal needs to include:

- Increasing the media's attention and advocacy
- Creating heightened visibility in the community, regionally, or nationally
- Soliciting donations of in-kind services or products
- Increasing volunteerism
- Providing outreach and education
- Building support of policy-makers and community influencers
- Attracting top staff and board members

Media Awareness

Though we discuss a variety of elements that might be encompassed within a cause-marketing partnership, we recommend centering the program on media relations. A media campaign can build ongoing awareness for both parties and achieve both parties' pre-determined goals. Thus, media can be the value proposition for the right cause partner and the crux of a cause-marketing partnership. These days, a strong emphasis on the Web—including social media, online public relations, search-engine marketing, search-engine optimization, blogging, and social bookmarking sites—is crucial. Without question, many non-profit groups are as hungry for media attention as their for-profit counterparts—sometimes even more so. As we mentioned in Step Two, today it is *de rigueur* for corporations to involve themselves in mainstream and highly publicized causes, such as breast-cancer research. These non-profit giants dominate the spotlight while other equally worthy causes fight for recognition and try to stay afloat.

Consider the Facts

Heart disease, not breast cancer, is the leading killer among women. Yet, for the past decade, non-profit groups devoted to breast-cancer research and breast-cancer awareness command far more media attention and raise far more than their counterparts focused on heart disease. We have seen a turnaround in media attention as organizations impacting heart disease are finally opening their eyes and fighting back with public relations campaigns of their own. However, they cannot rely on politicians' spouses or celebrities (or Heart Awareness Month) to generate sustained awareness and behavioral change. They must attract smart cause partners and take a grassroots approach in order to correct the trend and educate the public.

By providing a strategic public relations media campaign, a for-profit corporation can help a non-profit partner capture a part of this coveted online and traditional media attention. As public sentiment shifts to embrace the up-and-coming charitable organization (or a long-ignored cause or issue that has merit), the cause will enjoy larger donations and increased volunteerism.

Volunteerism

Though some non-profit groups operate primarily through the efforts of a paid staff, most charitable organizations are at least supplemented by volunteers, each of whom donates a few hours a week stuffing envelopes, answering phones, physically helping those in need, fundraising, or responding to donor requests for information. Often, a more skilled work force of volunteers is called upon for higher-level responsibilities. Accountants might donate their services *pro bono* to the charity of their choice. Attorneys regularly donate their services to non-profit clients, as do public relations firms such as ours. Medical doctors and physicians around the world are often called upon to assist those charities that provide care to underserved areas—from the well-known Doctors Without Borders to the lesser known non-profit groups such as the Next Right Thing, a California-based non-profit organization that connects doctors with needy children from third-world countries.

Non-profit groups are hungry for volunteers in any form, from the skilled worker to the line employee with few post-high school skills. With this in mind, a corporation can greatly help its cause partner by donating its employees' time to meet the non-profit's goals. A 50-person company can provide the equivalence of a full-time employee by donating one hour per week per employee to the non-profit cause.

The know-how brought to a non-profit group from its for-profit partner's executives and volunteers is also appealing. As discussed earlier, many non-profit leaders may not be up to date on the latest business strategies, systems, management tools, and technologies. Instead, they are working on tight budgets, cutting corners, and using bare-bones methods and antiquated equipment to get the job done.

One of our clients, a supermarket chain, partnered with a local non-profit group with limited staff resources, volunteers, and finances; the non-profit entity's headquarters were in physical disarray. Piles of paperwork were unattended. With such scattered and restricted resources, the non-profit group had few systems in place; its staff wasted hours shuffling through paperwork and trying to locate files. The supermarket chain responded by offering an administrative volunteer from its corporate offices to establish a filing system in the non-profit entity's headquarters. Within three months, the non-profit group was organized and efficient. This went far to solidify the partnership, which generated millions of media impressions each year for more than six consecutive years.

Another of our clients partnered with a non-profit group that had a computer and networking system circa 1998. With antiquated technology that required the non-profit group's staff to reboot the server (at least) daily, electronic processing was a challenge to say the least. Fortunately, its corporate partner not only donated a state-of-the-art computer system, but it also provided one of its in-house technology specialists who volunteered to help the non-profit partner design its network. Limited by a small budget, the non-profit group could have never afforded these services, much less the hardware necessary to design the sophisticated systems infrastructure.

A beauty-products client donated beauticians and products to assist underprivileged women re-entering the work force after taking time off to raise families. The volunteer beauticians provided beauty advice and instruction on how the women could look and feel their best. Our scuba-products client offered online fundraising and ongoing awareness to the Coral Reef Alliance, an outstanding environment cause.

When Habitat for Humanity was an up-and-comer, we partnered our engineering and architectural firm client with them, and the firm's employees took time from work to help build houses. The media coverage which we secured helped the cause, boosted employee morale, and increased staff productivity, which more than offset the man-hours which the firm donated to the cause.

Outreach and Education

Included within the goals of most non-profit groups is a commitment to educate the public and disseminate information central to the non-profit entity's mission. Cure Autism Now (CAN), a Los Angeles-based non-profit group that seeks research and manpower to find answers for autism "sooner rather than later," includes education and outreach as its goals.

CAN is not alone. Non-profit groups are given tax-exempt status because they all share a primary objective of supporting an issue with public benefit or of public concern. What about an issue that affects many people yet hasn't received the attention it deserves? This is an instance when cause marketing can help by enabling the non-profit partner to share its goals, purpose, or needs with the public and with its potential supporters. However, exploring a cause partner's willingness to go the extra mile is paramount. CAN is not always willing to do this because of the limitations which its board imposes, so cause selection requires in-depth research.

A for-profit advocate proposing a cause-marketing partnership with a non-profit group should take steps to address this objective. Our clients have helped their non-profit partners educate the public and conduct outreach by executing media events, including their mission and messages on printed materials, point-of-purchase signage, their website, in-school awareness efforts, and the like.

What You Get

Addressing the non-profit entity's objectives is necessary to ensure a complementary relationship between the non-profit and for-profit partners. As previously discussed, in a true partnership, both can benefit from the relationship. Learning the cause's goals helps determine synergies and establishes a foundation for the alliance. By engaging in activities (e.g., outreach, volunteerism, strategizing, etc.) that extend beyond media awareness, a for-profit corporation builds deep roots with its non-profit partner which not only helps forge a lasting relationship but also builds upon the campaign's authenticity.

Yet in its haste to engage the non-profit partner of its choice, a corporation should make sure that it keeps its own objectives in mind. If the non-profit partner is not interested in media attention, the for-profit corporation will not meet its objectives of improved visibility, credibility, and a bolstered image. If employee morale is a top corporate priority, a charity that does not want or need volunteers from the for-profit's staff might be a bad fit.

The Need for Mutual Need

Before meeting with your potential partner, revisit your objectives and consider those activities in which you want your non-profit partner to participate. At a minimum, you want your non-profit partner to be "hungry" for media attention. If the non-profit group is prone to shy away from newspaper and broadcast media or makes it difficult to secure its participation in media events, find another partner. When it is revealed that a potential charity partner wants to limit media exposure, heed the warning. Red flags could include the non-profit group's wanting to:

- Limit the number of media events it agrees to hold in conjunction with its corporate advocate. A cause partner that immediately begins placing a cap on the amount of time it will engage in media relations is not a smart fit. A for-profit partner will not achieve success or brand awareness if it is forced to halt its media activities because the cause has pulled the plug. Understanding that a shift in public perception happens over time, not overnight, both for-profit and non-profit partners should agree to consistently layer information and images on an ongoing basis.
- Limit activities to fundraising. A savvy non-profit group knows that it must create awareness to achieve its mission. Though raising money is critical, its goal is to affect positive change in its community. If a non-profit entity fails to think creatively and continues to suggest activities that are based only on fundraising, it likely does not appreciate the importance of media attention, and it will not be prone to engage enthusiastically in media events, social media, writing op-ed pieces, and other publicity opportunities.

Furthermore, do not overlook the obvious; be sure to consider the charity's geographical boundaries or limitations when selecting a partner. If you are a national company and need national attention, it may not make sense to select a purely local non-profit partner. If you are a local company seeking local or regional visibility, this obviously would not pose an issue. Many national non-profit groups can be inflexible and difficult to work with because of red tape and the layers of approval needed to move things forward. However, local chapters of these national organizations—such as Boys and Girls Clubs, Habitat for Humanity, and United Way—are often surprisingly nimble and accommodating, so explore the opportunities before accepting or rejecting such a charity.

Reciprocal Advocacy

When establishing your relationship, also consider whether the non-profit partner is willing to reciprocate by advocating your business. This is not by any means a requirement in the world of cause marketing. Under the model which my own company has historically implemented, the for-profit partner advocates the charity and creates heightened visibility for both organizations concurrently as the primary advantage to engaging in the relationship. Yet, in the more progressive cause-marketing models which we are implementing today, the partnership is reciprocal in that both the non-profit and the for-profit partners advocate the other to their respective constituents, donors, clients, or customers.

What do we mean by "reciprocal advocacy"? Let me give you an example.

We recently consulted with a national upscale retailer opening a new store in a wealthy, suburban community. Our plan was to partner the retailer with a local performing-arts center that had a database of past and present donors (theater-goers) that exceeded 100,000, most of whom were affluent and local. As part of the agreement forged between the retailer (for-profit) and the theater (non-profit), the theater was responsible for sending several

If the non-profit group is prone to shy away from newspaper and broadcast media or makes it difficult to secure its participation in media events, find another partner.

communiqués to its proprietary list announcing the retailer's grand opening. The theater urged those on its mailing list to support the retailer during its opening weekend, which in turn would help sustain the arts center. This was a mutually beneficial partnership in which both parties saw dividends. On opening weekend, the retail store's parking lot was jammed, and the company surpassed weekend sales projections by nearly 20 percent.

Online advocacy through e-newsletters, websites, social media sites, online communities, and blogs can be extremely beneficial, particularly when dealing with a target audience with a great deal of connectivity. Mommy Blogs—weblogs written by mothers for other parents—are one example of positive word-of-mouth.

A non-profit partner unwilling to advocate a corporation is not necessarily a deal-breaker. Many non-profit groups closely protect their donor lists—and for good reason. You may be fortunate enough to find a cause partner which will share its mailing list. After all, the media impressions created by a successful cause-marketing campaign are generally in the millions, far outweighing any lost opportunities due to a non-profit partner that is unwilling to advocate for you in return.

Creating a High Level of Engagement

More important than advocacy is the charity's willingness to fully engage in the partnership at the highest level. Your relationship with the non-profit group should begin and remain with the CEO or executive director. Before engaging a non-profit group in a cause-marketing partnership, request a meeting with the decision-maker and receive assurance that the group will remain involved and accessible. The media work on deadlines, and, if a campaign is placed on hold while a non-profit partner's board of directors considers a media opportunity or micromanages a press release, the partnership will surely lose important opportunities. As with large, bureaucratic companies, non-profit groups often act slowly. With a board of directors that meets infrequently, a non-profit entity might postpone important decisions until all members can discuss the potential partnership. If the executive director of the non-profit partner is willing to immediately push an item and, if necessary, call for an unscheduled board of directors or marketing committee meeting, you will save your partnership from losing valuable media attention.

On the same note, if your partner is a local chapter of a national charity, inquire ahead of time about the organization's relationship with its national or international parent organization. Some local charities are required to report to the national organization, which may insist on approving all such strategic alliances. Though having access to the national organization and all of its local chapters is a plus for any corporation, a non-profit entity's ties with its national headquarters can slow down an otherwise brilliant media campaign. Of course, as previously mentioned, all for-profit groups have different geographical goals and needs. This being said, all non-profit entities have unique structures and requirements. Save yourself from surprises by inquiring about your potential partner's structure in advance.

The Tab

In almost all cause-marketing relationships, the corporation is responsible for picking up the marketing program's tab. Like a successful marriage, it should be an equal partnership, with both parties gaining from the relationship. Bear in mind that the distribution of work and financial responsibility might seem disparate, but the outcome should be equally rewarding. Though the corporation might be charged with not only paying the bill but also determining strategy, counseling, and providing man-hours to the relationship, both non-profit and for-profit entities should realize value. Otherwise, the relationship turns into philanthropy and does not grow awareness for the cause—as in a cause-marketing effort. Though we applaud those willing to volunteer time, effort, or money to the world, cause-related marketing requires a commitment to more strategic considerations.

Formalizing the Agreement

Once you have compared objectives with your potential non-profit partner and have determined that the collaboration makes sound strategic sense, put the general terms of your agreement in writing. Though a formal contract might not be necessary, we suggest outlining the program in order to establish reasonable expectations. This helps avoid misunderstandings down the line.

Chapter 5:

Developing a Plan & Implementing Your Cause-Marketing Campaign

When it comes to increasing a company's bottom line, image, or employee morale, doing good is not enough. Old-school techniques, such as donating a percentage of profits or wearing a pink ribbon to denote support of a cause, have moved over to make way for more contemporary strategies for expressing a company's philanthropic side. Corporations that want to benefit from their socially responsible behavior must actively solicit attention and public awareness through a smart cause-marketing plan that includes grassroots media events, online advocacy, and word-of-mouth to communicate the cause involvement.

In this chapter, we discuss media events and related activities that help companies meet their objectives. This marks the exciting part of the journey, when theory, vision, and strategy converge. As companies start seeing the payoff— increasing employee morale, building awareness, and ultimately boosting the bottom line— they become increasingly dedicated to both their cause partner and the cause-marketing effort.

That said, every cause-related marketing program is different, requiring a unique agenda to help the partners actualize their goals. This chapter discusses not only these variable activities but also the activities germane to every cause-marketing campaign, namely media relations and the strategies, tactics, and pictures necessary to garner coverage, such as securing a prominent spokesperson and preparing the press materials required for a successful program.

Cause Marketing and Media Relations

The communally held goal of any cause-marketing campaign is securing coveted media attention. Public-relations and corporate-communications executives alike work to hone the story and disseminate a company's good news. With this powerful tool, a business that engages in a non-profit partnership to forward its agenda by becoming a *bona fide* advocate of a cause and clearly showing genuine concern for it, has an excellent chance of securing media attention, and can offer an even better story to tell the public.

So the question remains: How does a cause partnership secure media attention when numerous equally worthy stories are competing for the same time, space, or attention? Addressing this problem requires a basic understanding of the media. The press's approach to storytelling serves as the model for the company's approach to pitching stories to the media.

Layering the Media with Information

Some companies make the mistake of providing the media with a bulky press kit filled with endless information that has not been requested. In a world dominated by information clutter and deadlines, who in the press has time for this? Like the rest of us, members of the media are overwhelmed with paperwork on a daily basis, sifting through piles of press releases, media advisories, e-mails, electronic media kits, and urgent requests for coverage. They are often hard-pressed to cover the general-news events, let alone spend long hours pouring over your company's history, background, and key executives' bios, as well as the equivalent amount of information from your cause-partner counterpart. The solution is to send a short pitch letter to ensure that each of you gets their attention, then offer a follow-up letter to convince them of the merits of the story (and pictures). We know it is important not to waste the media's limited time, so we always communicate the eye-catching headline, the hottest news, a great photo op, or offer high-impact differentiators.

Layering messages to the media is vitally important in the education process because the media can, in turn, educate people about the cause and what the for-profit partner is doing to aid the organization. Therefore, a commitment to an enduring program is the key to any strategic cause-related marketing effort. At a minimum, the layers of information should include:

- A news release for widespread distribution and media relations
- A kickoff event for a "mediagenic" launch
- Media alerts for subsequent creative media events that will continue to raise awareness of the partnership
- A news release announcing the amount of money generated by the cause
- Media communiqués alerting the press about "feel-good" (human-interest) stories that the partnership has allowed the cause to realize (pitch letters are optimal vehicles to get media attention)
- Op-ed pieces in the for-profit partner's name regarding the efficacy of the cause and the importance of being a good corporate citizen
- Online news-release distribution

- Online news-outlet relations, including social media and bloggers

Before we discuss the details of creating clever events, let's first talk about the media alerts and news releases necessary to promote an event or partnership.

Draft a Compelling News Release

Media alerts (also known as media advisories), which are used to announce events, and news releases (also known as press releases), which are used to announce non-event information, must be "hot." They must get the attention of the media and do so quickly and effectively within the headline and first paragraph. Therefore, the lead must be intriguing and evoke interest. Media alerts and news releases, like news stories, are written by starting with a "hot hook" in the first sentence and more detailed, specific information following in order of importance. This structure serves two purposes. First, it provides readers with immediate information. Most experts agree that an advertiser has only a second or two to catch a person's attention. The same is true when trying to garner attention from the press. Confusing, long-winded, difficult-to-read press communiqués do little to draw in a reader.

The key to an effective release or advisory is to keep it short, simple, and dynamic. In other words, use the press as a model. Are you more likely to read three articles of 100 words accompanied by several great photos or five more detailed stories of 1,000 words and no photos? If the message is long and confusing, you will likely move on to another story. We are a USAToday.com universe, so be concise.

We strongly suggest limiting all releases and alerts to one page, with a maximum length of one and one-half pages, and sending them to several media contacts at each news outlet, depending upon the story.

The components of your media advisory/press release should include the:

- Headline
- Lead sentence and timely tie-in
- Spokesperson's quotation (optional)
- Details of the story (paint the picture)
- Boilerplate

We'll discuss these one at a time.

Headline

Most important in drafting an alert or release is a vibrant headline followed by a captivating lead sentence. Intriguing headlines use small but powerful words. Though your colleges might be impressed by your prolific vocabulary, the general public may be disinclined to read on; indeed, reporters are taught to write in a style that sixth-graders can understand. This does not mean that your headline should be written in a sophomoric fashion, but rather so it can be easily and quickly understood. Do not make the reader dig for definitions. Now is not the time to display your well-established and poetic prose. It is, however, a good opportunity to tie in a topical issue, use a clever play on words, or make a statement that pulls in the reader. Your headline should arouse curiosity.

A boring headline:

SEEING EYE FOUNDATION KICKS OFF PARTNERSHIP WITH RACECAR DRIVER

This headline is informative, but it does not paint a vivid picture, and it is far from compelling. In addition, we recommend ignoring conventional "wisdom" and the over-used inclusion of corporate names in headlines (unless you are required to adhere to SEC regulations for publicly traded companies). We often use a sub-head to further paint the picture. This point should be clear: The headline is the most important sentence or phrase in a news release or media advisory.

A strong headline:
BLIND WOMAN WITH DOG IN HER LAP
DRIVES LAP IN RACECAR

Simple and to the point, this headline arouses curiosity. Why is a dog, much less a blind woman, in a racecar? Did this occur during an official race? Who was really driving? All of these unanswered questions pull the reader into the story.

The Lead Sentence

The same sentiment—short and dynamic—can be carried to the lead sentence, which is the second most important component of your advisory or release. Within this sentence, quickly and simply address some or all of the five W's of reporting: who, what, where, when, and why. Your lead sentence also determines whether the rest of the communiqué is going to be read, so being able to answer the following questions affirmatively is extremely important. Is it easy to read? Does it use active verbs? Is it simple, yet informative? Does it arouse curiosity?

If writing is not your *forte*, spend some time reading newspapers. Notice that most leads are short, general, and dynamic. Notice that they contain the most important information of the story and that they raise enough curiosity to keep the reader's interest. Because the purpose of a release or advisory is to attract media attention, and the media—including radio, which must paint aural pictures to a listening, visualizing audience—use a visual medium, you should always start with a sentence that promises a strong photo opportunity.

A boring lead:

"Mary Jones, a blind woman who works for the Seeing Eye Foundation, and her seeing-eye dog, Spot, are going to join racecar driver Mark Smith to drive around the Meadowlands Racetrack on Tuesday at 11:00 a.m."

Hard to read, confusing, and filled with too many details, this lead bogs down the reader and fails to incite interest. Though answering the five W's is important, which the lead does, its failure to intrigue the reader by providing too much information in the lead sentence is a big mistake.

A strong lead:

"Join a blind woman and her dog as they speed along the Meadowlands Racetrack on Tuesday."

Answering all five W's in general terms, this is a short, 16-word hot lead which contains only four words exceeding two syllables. It provides enough information to engage the reader but not so much that the reader is disinclined to continue reading because of information overload. Importantly, it arouses curiosity. The readers still want to know why the blind woman and her dog will be in a racecar. They want details, which means they want to keep reading. Finally, it promises a unique photo opportunity.

Some writers have a tendency to "bury the lead" three or four sentences into the release or advisory, instead setting the reader up for further disclosure a few sentences down. While opening with a dynamic story or quote can be effective, building up to the lead is generally considered a mistake. Though we are not entirely opposed to breaking the rules, we do believe that one must first master the rule before breaking it. Unless you have secured the expertise of a media strategist, we suggest you use the aforementioned formula. Start with a strong lead and, if applicable, follow it with the expert testimonial or topical news that ties in with your story.

The Spokesperson

Soon after the lead, consider introducing the campaign's spokesperson by quoting her/him. The spokesperson should be a key executive well versed on the relationship, prepared to liaison with the media, and armed with a genuine, personal story connecting the spokesperson to the cause. Generally, the spokesperson is the same person whose contact details are included in the press kit representing the corporate partner outlined in the boilerplate (discussed below). When working with clients, we require the spokesperson to be a key executive of the for-profit organization rather than a hired gun. Since one of the primary objectives of a cause-marketing partnership is to increase brand awareness for the company, assigning a corporate spokesperson allows both the non-profit and the for-profit groups to receive face time. The for-profit spokesperson relates his/her company name while discussing the non-profit entity and their partnership. If the spokesperson is a representative of the non-profit partner rather than the company, the for-profit partner might very well be left out of the equation. In many instances, a spokesperson from both entities will be interviewed.

The decision to include a quotation from the spokesperson

should be made on a case-by-case basis. If you do decide to include a quotation from the spokesperson, make sure that it is not only clever but also summarizes the differentiators, reveals interesting information, or is controversial. Remember to get the media's attention at all times.

A boring quotation:

"The Seeing Eye is a good cause, and I'm proud to sponsor it," said Mark Smith.

Aside from failing to identify the speaker's relationship with the cause, this quotation does not say anything exciting, nor does it contain any personal element. Simply put, it is boring.

A strong quotation:

"Racing cars is about feeling—not sight: the feeling of the wind, the rush of exhilaration, the way your heartbeat increases with speed," said Mark Smith, the Indianapolis 500 racecar driver who will carry Mary Jones and her seeing-eye dog as passengers in his car.

This quote promotes both Smith and the cause, while providing a personal connection to Smith and inviting the reader to imagine how a blind individual experiences the exciting sensation of racing.

The Details

By now, you have aroused curiosity, promoted your organization by quoting a spokesperson, and revealed interesting information. You have also created the foundation for a strong image—the most important part of the advisory or release—by specifying a media-friendly activity. The release/advisory has hooked the reader, so now you can start providing details.

Smith, an advocate of The Seeing Eye, was almost unable to fulfill his lifelong dream of racing cars due to an eyesight issue of his own. As *part of his commitment to the cause, Mark will escort Mary and Spot on a 180-mph sprint around the Meadowlands Racetrack. Smith has continued to advocate this cause, donating a percentage of his earnings this year—$60,000—to The Seeing Eye.*

The mission of The Seeing Eye is to enhance the independence, dignity, and self-confidence of blind people through the use of Seeing Eye dogs.

If you are sending an advisory (as opposed to a press release, which is more informational), remember to also provide the *who, what, why, when, and where,* in bold, bulleted format just after the headline.

Who: A seeing eye dog named Spot; Mary Jones, who is blind but was given a new lease on life because of Spot; Indy Car driver Mark Smith; Seeing Eye Foundation President John Doe

Why: To elevate awareness of the Seeing Eye and promote advocacy and support of this important cause

What: Smith takes seeing-eye dog and Mary Jones in his racecar to 180mph *to feel* the exhilaration of the auto-racing experience

Where: Meadowlands Raceway, Meadowlands Sports Complex

When: Tuesday, September 2, at 11 a.m.

Boilerplate

The boilerplate simply provides concise background and contact information in one short paragraph regarding each of the cause partners.

Formatting

Smart news releases and media advisories follow a certain format. They are usually written in lines separated by one and one-half inches of spacing, are created in an easy-to-read font such as Arial, and are not longer than one page. The top of the release includes the phrase "For Immediate Release" or "News Release" and ends with "###," a symbol understood to mean "The End."

Photo Opportunity

In crafting a media advisory or alert designed to encourage all the press to attend an event, it is vital to ensure that the media can clearly envision the photo opportunity. Simply publicizing a commencement ceremony is not enough. The media do not know whether this will be a formal gathering held at a podium with two people shaking hands or a giant check that is being presented (both events are fairly common and are extremely boring, and neither is mediagenic), or if the kickoff will be accompanied by an exciting chance to take unique, dynamic pictures. If the photo opportunity is unclear, rewrite your media alert.

If you are merely announcing the partnership without inviting the press to an event, hire someone to take a candid and engaging "news" photo that can accompany the release, alerting the press as to the various photo opportunities that exist should they choose to cover the story and dig more deeply into the relationship.

Let's look at the media alerts and news releases which we sent to the media for Mark Smith and The Seeing Eye Foundation.

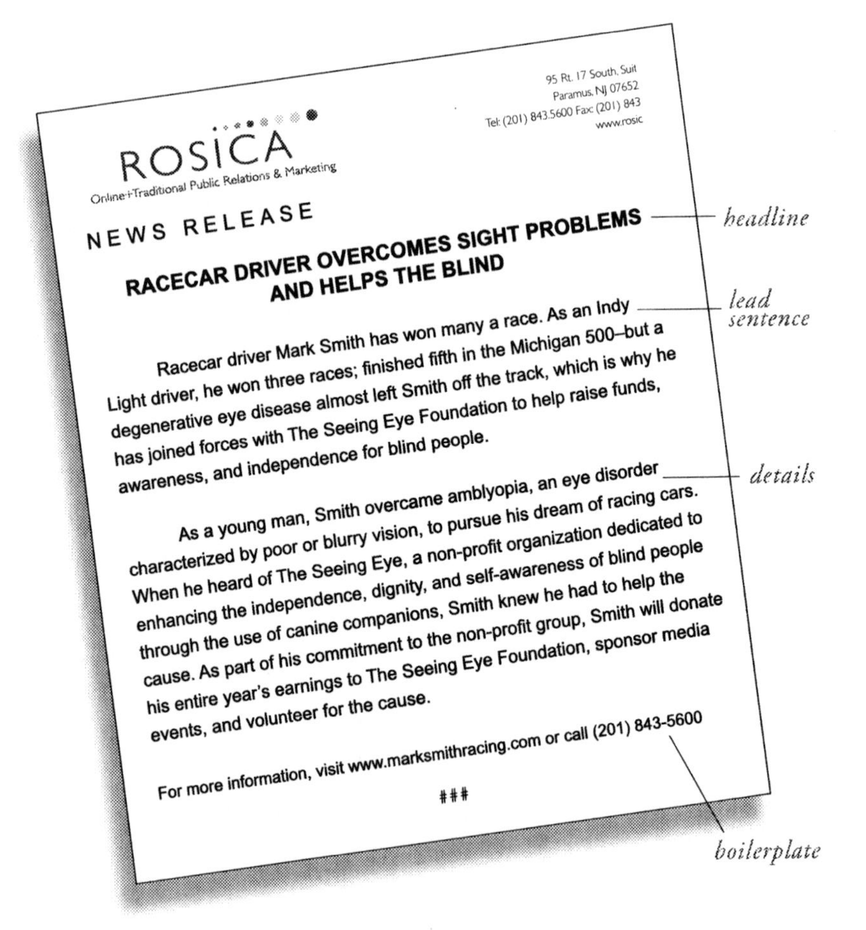
95 Rt. 17 South, Suit
Paramus, NJ 07652
Tel: (201) 843.5600 Fax: (201) 843
www.rosic

ROSICA
Online+Traditional Public Relations & Marketing

NEWS RELEASE

RACECAR DRIVER OVERCOMES SIGHT PROBLEMS AND HELPS THE BLIND

Racecar driver Mark Smith has won many a race. As an Indy Light driver, he won three races; finished fifth in the Michigan 500–but a degenerative eye disease almost left Smith off the track, which is why he has joined forces with The Seeing Eye Foundation to help raise funds, awareness, and independence for blind people.

As a young man, Smith overcame amblyopia, an eye disorder characterized by poor or blurry vision, to pursue his dream of racing cars. When he heard of The Seeing Eye, a non-profit organization dedicated to enhancing the independence, dignity, and self-awareness of blind people through the use of canine companions, Smith knew he had to help the cause. As part of his commitment to the non-profit group, Smith will donate his entire year's earnings to The Seeing Eye Foundation, sponsor media events, and volunteer for the cause.

For more information, visit www.marksmithracing.com or call (201) 843-5600

###

This release, which announced Smith's partnership with The Seeing Eye, was accompanied by a photo of Smith in his racing gear while petting a seeing-eye dog. It landed Smith on the cover of Parade Magazine.

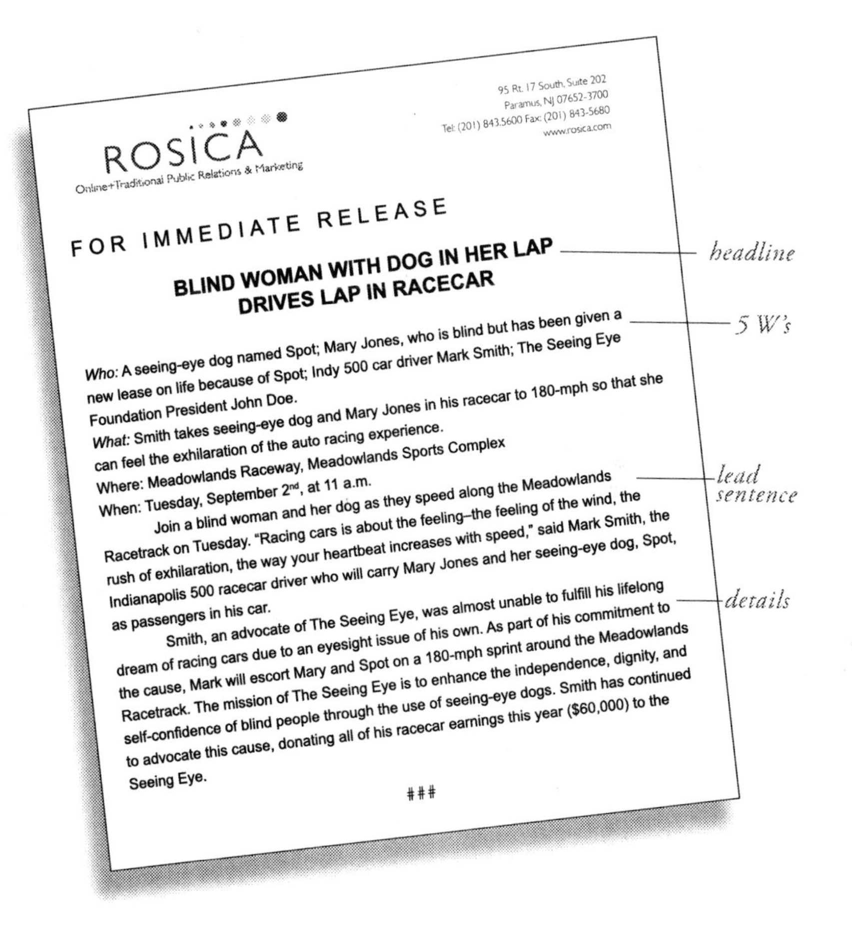

ROSICA
Online+Traditional Public Relations & Marketing

95 Rt. 17 South, Suite 202
Paramus, NJ 07652-3700
Tel: (201) 843.5600 Fax: (201) 843-5680
www.rosica.com

FOR IMMEDIATE RELEASE

BLIND WOMAN WITH DOG IN HER LAP DRIVES LAP IN RACECAR

Who: A seeing-eye dog named Spot; Mary Jones, who is blind but has been given a new lease on life because of Spot; Indy 500 car driver Mark Smith; The Seeing Eye Foundation President John Doe.
What: Smith takes seeing-eye dog and Mary Jones in his racecar to 180-mph so that she can feel the exhilaration of the auto racing experience.
Where: Meadowlands Raceway, Meadowlands Sports Complex
When: Tuesday, September 2nd, at 11 a.m.

Join a blind woman and her dog as they speed along the Meadowlands Racetrack on Tuesday. "Racing cars is about the feeling–the feeling of the wind, the rush of exhilaration, the way your heartbeat increases with speed," said Mark Smith, the Indianapolis 500 racecar driver who will carry Mary Jones and her seeing-eye dog, Spot, as passengers in his car.

Smith, an advocate of The Seeing Eye, was almost unable to fulfill his lifelong dream of racing cars due to an eyesight issue of his own. As part of his commitment to the cause, Mark will escort Mary and Spot on a 180-mph sprint around the Meadowlands Racetrack. The mission of The Seeing Eye is to enhance the independence, dignity, and self-confidence of blind people through the use of seeing-eye dogs. Smith has continued to advocate this cause, donating all of his racecar earnings this year ($60,000) to the Seeing Eye.

###

Media alert announcing event, again accompanied by photo of Smith in his racing gear, this time inside his car with a dog at the wheel.

95 Rt. 17 South, Suit
Paramus, NJ 07652
Tel: (201) 843.5600 Fax: (201) 843
www.rosic

ROSICA
Online+Traditional Public Relations & Marketing

NEWS RELEASE

RACECAR DRIVER TAKES BLIND WOMAN AND SEEING EYE DOG ACROSS FINISHING LINE — *headline*

This is no ordinary "lap" dog

It matters not to Indianapolis 500 racecar driver Mark Smith whether he wins his next race; Smith knows that he and his "pet" cause, The Seeing Eye Foundation have already won. — *lead sentence*

Following Tuesday's event at the Meadowlands Racetrack in which Smith escorted a blind woman, Mary Jones, and her seeing-eye dog on a 180–mph sprint around the track. The Seeing Eye was bequeathed $1 million from an anonymous source. Smith, an advocate of The Seeing Eye, was almost unable to fulfill his lifelong dream of racing cars due to an eyesight issue of his own. As part of the commitment to the cause, Smith has donated his racecar earnings this year to The Seeing Eye. His generosity, coupled with the $1 million donation, brought an ecstatic reaction from the Seeing Eye Foundation. — *details*

"Up until last week, nothing beat the rush of exhilaration that accompanied a sprint around the track. But now, I'd say that nothing beats the feeling of helping a deserving cause help thousands of people" said Smith.

###

Post-event news release, accompanied by a photo taken of Smith, Jones, and Spot at the media event.

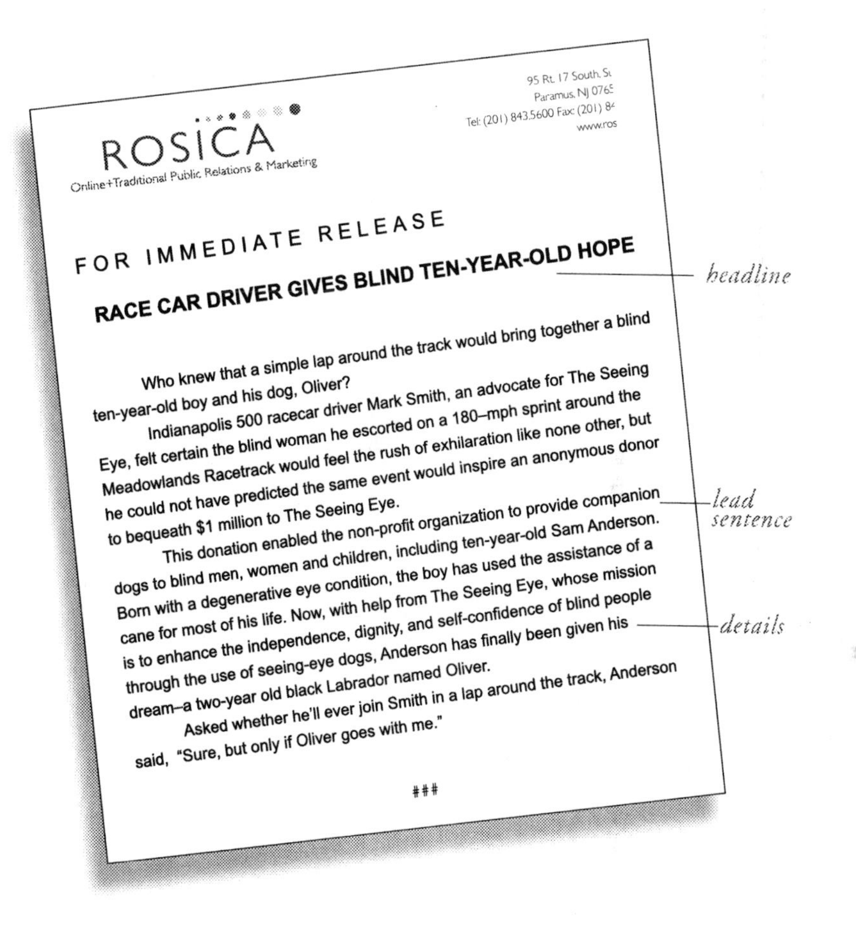

FOR IMMEDIATE RELEASE

RACE CAR DRIVER GIVES BLIND TEN-YEAR-OLD HOPE

Who knew that a simple lap around the track would bring together a blind ten-year-old boy and his dog, Oliver?

Indianapolis 500 racecar driver Mark Smith, an advocate for The Seeing Eye, felt certain the blind woman he escorted on a 180–mph sprint around the Meadowlands Racetrack would feel the rush of exhilaration like none other, but he could not have predicted the same event would inspire an anonymous donor to bequeath $1 million to The Seeing Eye.

This donation enabled the non-profit organization to provide companion dogs to blind men, women and children, including ten-year-old Sam Anderson. Born with a degenerative eye condition, the boy has used the assistance of a cane for most of his life. Now, with help from The Seeing Eye, whose mission is to enhance the independence, dignity, and self-confidence of blind people through the use of seeing-eye dogs, Anderson has finally been given his dream–a two-year old black Labrador named Oliver.

Asked whether he'll ever join Smith in a lap around the track, Anderson said, "Sure, but only if Oliver goes with me."

###

News release announcing outcomes, accompanied by a photo taken of Smith with a child and a seeing-eye dog.

Checklist for Crafting Attention-Getting News Releases/Media Alerts

- Is your headline attention-getting? Does it make you want to read the copy? Is it in 14-point font?
- Is there a sub-head?
- If announcing an event, does your media advisory start with the five W's in bulleted form?
- Does your lead sentence spark interest and paint a compelling picture, identifying the five W's?
- If a media advisory is offered, is the photo op clear and does it demand attention?
- Does the release/advisory start with the most important information presented first, with supporting information and details at the end?
- Is the advisory/release one to one and one-half pages in length at most?
- Is it presented in lines separated by one and one-half spaces, using 12-point font in the body?
- Has someone other than you, its author, proofread the entire copy for grammar, punctuation, and style?
- Have you used active verbs throughout?
- Does it follow proper formatting?
- Does it demand attention?

Crafting Clever Media Events

Everyone, from participant to onlooker, agrees that a ribbon-cutting ceremony is a yawn. So is the seemingly obligatory giant-check presentation, which is why the media rarely cover such events. They want something fresh and exciting, and a cause-marketing partnership must create events that will pique interest if it wants to realize its objectives.

No matter how strong the media advisory, the media will not attend an event that does not promise a strong photo opportunity. Creating a good picture as described on pages 97–103 should be the driving force behind the media event, and all plans to secure media attention should include a description of what photo ops will be available.

As we discussed at length, the pink-ribbon campaign for Breast Cancer Awareness Month lacks freshness, so when our client, Big Bear Supermarket, joined forces with the Stefanie Spielman Fund for Breast Cancer Research, we were put to the test.

How do we create an original, mediagenic press opportunity? Our "Light up the Night in Pink" campaign urged citizens in Columbus, Ohio, to purchase pink light bulbs from Big Bear Supermarket during the month of October and replace their porch bulbs with the pink bulbs on the last night of Breast Cancer Awareness Month as a sign of solidarity. (Patrons stopping in to purchase the pink light bulbs also bought groceries from the supermarket.) On the evening of October 31, entire city blocks and neighborhoods showed their support for breast-cancer victims and survivors by "lighting up the night in pink." Media vans cruised neighborhoods to find the pinkest part of town and, in ensuing days, one broadcast station started a contest to find the neighborhood with the most consecutive number of pink homes. Our supermarket client's same-store sales jumped 17 percent in October and November over the prior year's sales.

Here's another example of a creative media event. We brought the beach to the city on a 50-foot flatbed truck filled with sand and beach equipment to help raise consciousness for Melanoma Awareness. Models applied sunscreen and children wore sun-protective clothing as our spokesperson communicated the campaign's message. The media responded with TV, radio, and newspaper coverage, resulting in 30 million media impressions in fewer than 60 days.

During a snowstorm in Denver, we launched a national ice cream brand and sampled the product "for literacy awareness." In the midst of the blizzard, our clients stood outside and asked those brave enough to weather the storm to sample a new ice cream to benefit literacy. For each sample taken, Borden's Foods donated a pre-determined dollar amount to the literacy cause which we had selected. The media loved the image of people eating ice cream in the middle of a snowstorm, and we effectively communicated the story because of the event's quirkiness.

And what better way to get the media's attention than to involve them in the event? For another supermarket client who partnered with the Children's Hunger Alliance, we invited news anchors to participate in a shopping-cart race through the supermarket to raise money for the charity. This secured for our client over an hour's worth of free media time on all four network affiliates over a 48-hour period.

As you can see, it requires creativity and strategy—but the cause affiliation has an important element that news media *want* to carry.

Television news anchors compete for more than ratings in a shopping-cart race through Big Bear Supermarket for the benefit of Children's Hunger Alliance.

Other Cause-Marketing Events

Included in the for-profit group's ability to sell the partnership as genuine is its dedication to engaging its employees. Though these activities can help a company reach objectives that are not directly geared toward the media, such as improving employee morale or improving a company's online reputation, a partnership would be remiss if it fails to promote these activities.

Whatever variable and additional media relations activities you might include in the partnership, which might be volunteerism, allocation of resources, or cash donations, be sure to take the opportunity to publicize these events not only to the media but also to your clients, stakeholders, and employees.

Reinforce the power of your cause-marketing message on a monthly basis by sending your key influencers links to positive online news coverage, videos, and blogs. Depending on the objectives of the campaign, we generally suggest that for-profit partners frequently communicate with their employees about any upcoming opportunities to get involved, as well as broadcast the results from the cause partnership. Smart for-profit corporations can recruit candidates for employment by executing effective public relations/cause-marketing campaigns and promoting the relationship on the Web.

The beach comes to the city to advance skin-cancer awareness.

By creating online awareness, companies also attract additional attention from potential customers and spread positive brand awareness.

The rule of thumb is this: Whatever you do, make it known as far and wide as possible. If the partnership receives media attention, send a letter to your client base with a clipping that details the partnership and link to the news article from your website. If you know that the partnership is going to be featured on the radio or television, send your clients an e-mail asking that they tune in, and be sure to keep in touch with the times using online publicity. Send links to blogs and news stories with positive coverage.

Online Media and Publicity

Opportunities abound online for spreading the word about cause marketing, and if your company is not embracing technology, it is missing one of the most effective and measurable methods of marketing today. In fact, in 2010, the number of Facebook users outnumbered the population of the United States

By sending information via the Internet, companies can elevate their visibility, improve their search-engine rankings, and drive traffic straight to their websites. Following are just some of the ways in which companies can use the Internet, social networking sites, their own websites and online distribution channels to promote their causes.

Publicizing a company's charitable involvement online can impact its page rank, because search engines, such as Google, elevate the importance of non-profit groups and those companies affiliated with charities. Non-profit involvement will be noticed by search-engine "spiders" that read, evaluate, and rank a website's importance on numerous variables and mathematical computations called algorithms. Algorithms are established to rank the millions of websites and create a hierarchy of relevant sites. Google's algorithm for ranking sites, for instance, weighs charities heavier than for-profit corporations, so, by linking to a company from a 501(c)3, a business's website may receive more visibility and be deemed more credible and valuable.

If a cause partnership receives media coverage, by all means, the corporation's website should highlight the media. Social bookmarking and social networking sites, including Twitter, Facebook, and YouTube, can be used to promote these positive stories. Search engines also see news sources as credible, and being mentioned on a media website will elevate a business's online visibility and bring it closer to the top of natural searches. In addition, social-media news releases are sure to increase in popularity as they continue to integrate copy, video, images, RSS feeds, social networking, and social bookmarking elements.

Many companies encourage their employees to act as good will ambassadors by posting information about their experiences on social networking sites such as, LinkedIn and Facebook. Online community bulletin boards are another outlet. In some cases, it might be appropriate to incentivize employees to help spread the message about their authentic participation with offers of an extra vacation day, free lunch, or another appealing perk.

Compelling pictures and videos can carry the message as well as, if not better than, words. The online photo management and sharing application Flickr, as well as the video-sharing through YouTube and other sites, can be deployed to convey a visual representation of a cause-marketing initiative and generate positive word-of-mouth. How about an entertaining video of staffers working at a mediagenic charity event? Judging by the most popularly viewed YouTube videos, people enjoy comedy, music, and dance the most. Anything that lends itself to capitalize on those tastes might produce a hit on YouTube. Of course, video and images should also be posted on the company's website and should be "optimized" for important keywords.

Social Media + Cause Marketing = Positive Online Reputation

The social-media communications channel can help broaden awareness and generate grassroots support. It can also be used to reach key influencers, such as consumers, elected officials, advocacy organizations, and other important groups. Using Facebook as a vehicle to promote your cause can be powerful, particularly when combined with other social-media tools, including YouTube, blogging on a company or CEO's blog, and Twitter. Properly promoting your social-media profiles in the content which you disseminate is critical, as are search-engine optimization (SEO) campaigns that can help your organization receive a higher page rank. SEO campaigns can also help you secure targeted Twitter followings of thousands of people.

Online reputation management through social media is also an important weapon in the fight against inaccurate, amateur, and misleading user-generated Web content. The volume of this unpredictable and unqualified information is growing exponentially, making it increasingly important for brands, companies and CEOs to take proactive measures in influencing the online conversation. This can be accomplished by engaging in online dialog while concurrently working to manage online content, particularly dominating the first two to three pages of searchers for key phrases specific to a company's products, services, or industries.

Technology is making content production more accessible and affordable to ordinary people through such services as PRWeb, a distribution channel used by more than 40,000 companies and organizations of all sizes to disseminate news releases and optimize searches. A company should make sure that its releases are optimized to help its search-engine ranking. Based on their Google Page Ranking, approximately 30 online news-release distribution sites are worth using.

Responding to the popularity of the social-messaging and micro-blogging service Twitter, PRWeb launched a feature called Tweetit that enables customers to automatically share their news through Twitter at the same time it is posted on PRWeb. An indication of the power of social messaging occurred in the immediate aftermath of the bombings in India's financial capital of Mumbai in November 2008. Mainstream media outlets struggled to convey the scope of the tragedy while Twitter users transmitted real-time accounts of the attacks.

Facebook, Twitter, Tweetit, PRWeb, blogs, Flickr, YouTube, LinkedIn, Bing, Yahoo, SEO—the list of available technologies is always growing. Know that your younger competitors, and many of your older competitors, are keeping up with the times. In fact, the share of adult Internet users over the age of 30 who have a profile on an online social-network site, such as Facebook, has more than quadrupled from 8 percent in 2005 to 40 percent at the end of 2009, according to the Pew Internet & American Life Project's 2009 tracking survey. If your company is not familiar with these technologies, hire a specialist immediately—or risk being left behind. We started Interact Marketing (www.Interact Marketing.com) in 2009 in response to the importance of these tools and the impact which these activities can have in promoting and protecting brands and companies alike.

Chapter 6:

Measuring Results

An effective cause-marketing campaign includes a plan to measure results as well as a strategy to shift activities if goals are not being met.

Evaluation tools play a significant role in any public relations or marketing effort; if you cannot measure the return on investment, such as an increase in sales, employee satisfaction, public perception, or brand awareness, then why conduct the marketing campaign in the first place? Today, technology makes measuring a campaign's success not only possible but also simple.

By continuing to relate back to the original purposes of a cause-marketing effort, companies are reminded of their objectives, making them more likely to stay on track or create a new path if goals are not being realized. As a reminder, most cause-marketing objectives fall into one or more of five categories:

- Increasing sales
- Increasing brand awareness
- Improving employee morale, including hiring, retention, and loyalty
- Preventing or managing crises and managing online reputation

- Creating a fresh publicity strategy

This chapter details the tools that allow a company to measure the success of its cause-marketing efforts in terms that relate to each of these objectives.

Increasing Sales

Throughout the book, we have discussed increased profit as the gold-standard objective in any cause-marketing effort. While this is true, an increase in sales is the simplest measurement standard available. But by simply looking at sales spikes or declines, a company can miss the cause-and-effect relationship of a cause-marketing campaign. The key to measuring the efficacy of a cause-related marketing effort is to determine whether a shift in sales is directly related to the program or whether an upward (or downward) trend is related to another micro or macro economic factor. The economy, a shift in product quality, or another change in a company's strategy, are other variables which can obviously impact sales.

The key word is specificity. Be sure to measure your sales results specifically in the market in which the cause-marketing campaign is being implemented so that local efforts are not measured by national standards. When Famous Amos founder, Wally Amos, became the national spokesperson for Literacy Volunteers of America, we collaborated to organize a chain of grassroots media events held at local libraries. After one of the initial events, held in the nation's capital, we measured sales specifically in Washington, D.C., and found that Famous Amos had enjoyed a 24-percent increase in sales in this demographic marketing area following our public relations blitz, which included a media event, morning show appearances, and a sampling promotion at a key retailer.

Quantify the results by using tools that capture where a lead was generated. This will be most accurate if you use online tools, such as lead capture or landing pages, with campaign-specific URLs and landing pages. Much of marketing's future is online and measurement is made easy using the Internet.

Online tools are modern measurement tactics which are the most effective and easiest to implement. They can track leads and accurately gauge a cause-marketing budget's return on investment. Combined with today's predominance of Internet-savvy consumers, tools for measuring results help a company make better decisions and amplify its results. How do these tools work?

A company can design landing pages—or micro-sites—for responses specific to media activities related to its cause-marketing program. Moreover, by creating a designated URL for its cause-marketing effort, the company can track the number of people responding solely by the interest which the campaign generates. Using such programs as Webtrends or Google Analytics, you can see when sales leads are generated by people who found your website through media websites or in response to an article, a TV segment, or a media event. (And, as we mentioned on page 153, media placements garnered through a cause-marketing effort will boost your online visibility by increasing your search-engine rankings.)

Following the online search trends related to your company can also help evaluate interest and demand for a company or brand as it is impacted through a cause-marketing campaign, or any strategic marketing initiative, for that matter. This might sound complicated, but such tracking is quick and easy to achieve with the help of an online marketing expert.

The benefits of website analytics extend beyond cause marketing. Internet marketing agencies such as Search Troop and Internet Marketing can readily implement tools that allow you to track such information and drive traffic to a site through SEO, e-mail, and other creative means. They generate results online and provide real-time measurement. The following strategies also help:

- Determine the source, cause marketing-related or otherwise, that attracted the customer, which allows you to best evaluate the return on investment for all of your marketing efforts.
- Capture each potential customer's information in order to develop a highly valuable database.
- Create viral marketing opportunities that help companies saturate the marketplace.
- Support efforts to protect a company or brand's online reputation.

Important to note is the considerable influence of industry websites, blogs, social-networking sites, discussion channels, video-sharing sites, and chat rooms, which continue to be valuable tools to optimally position companies high in natural search results and attract new adopters (who are more than likely to spread the word and tell the online community of their experience). Smart and effective practitioners understand how to integrate online and offline marketing. For a recently published article I wrote on this subject, visit www.rosica.com.

Building Brand Awareness

A company's ability to generate considerable brand awareness and loyal, even fanatical, customers feeds directly into its valuation. Generally speaking, known companies are worth considerably more than those that are unknown. Investors recognize that good will improves the value of a company because brand awareness, loyal customers, and greater potential for growth accompany it.

Though valuation is one tool for measuring a company's worth, standard appraisal tools might not consider the intangible values and brand equity created by a solid cause-marketing effort. *The Authentic Brand: How Today's Top Entrepreneurs Connect with Customers* discusses a dozen highly prominent entrepreneurs who embraced cause marketing early on and sold their businesses later for well above the rate justified by modern accounting practices and for much more than logic would have suggested.

For those companies who want a defined measure of a shift in brand awareness, we suggest retaining a research company such as Harris Interactive. In addition to its international presence and well-honed survey tools, Harris provides valuable counsel to help shape the major questions which a company should ask. Through Harris or a similar service that can generate a national probability sample or survey of a more defined target audience, a company can gauge brand awareness both before and during the cause-marketing campaign's execution, pinpointing how a specific program or media activity is impacting brand recognition. Survey tools can be tailored for geographical relevance, such as awareness in New England, nationally, or even globally, thus allowing companies to better understand where to focus their cause-marketing efforts in order to achieve a maximum return.

Even a company with limited resources can afford this service, which measures fluctuations in brand awareness (knowledge of the company, its products/services, and its philanthropic efforts). Smart corporations also evaluate the perception they have created by asking questions that extract the brand essence—that word or phrase which comes to mind when people think of their company. Similar surveys can be taken with existing or potential customers who fall within a company's target demographic. These marketing-effectiveness studies can be done online, via telephone, or at trade shows and might include questions such as the following:

- Have you heard of [Company X]?
- If so, what does [Company X] do?
- Are you aware of [Company X's] philanthropic involvement?
- What one word or phrase comes to mind with respect to [Company X]?
- What causes are you passionate about?

After six or twelve months, with periodic repetitions thereafter, companies should conduct another survey with existing customers to see if and how their perceptions of the company have continued to change throughout the cause-marketing campaign. The following is a model for this survey:

- Have you heard about [Company X's] involvement with [Charity Y]?
- Knowing that [Company X] is involved with [Charity Y], would you be more or less likely to consider [Company X] as your service/product provider [describe service/product]?
- Would you be interested in receiving additional news in the future regarding [Company X's] involvement with [Charity Y]?
- What one word or phrase comes to mind with respect to [Company X]?
- What causes are you passionate about?

Another tool for measuring the brand awareness of a company is to track the increase in *repeat* business. For best results, if you are not already doing so, start measuring repeat customers before kicking off the campaign. Based on the logistics of your business, consider creating a strategy for determining how often repeat clients should purchase from you, taking into consideration how customers are impacted by your selling cycle and the normal reordering time period for your most regular clients. Retailers can easily measure the loyalty response and compare against pre-cause campaign numbers.

Website traffic, again via a specified micro-site designed to track traffic motivated by the cause partnership and to generate specific action, is among the most effective ways to track brand awareness. By using the affordable Web tracking tools described earlier, or by hiring a company that specializes in Internet marketing and SEO, companies can integrate their cause-marketing programs with Internet marketing's measurement benefits. Search engines, particularly Google, favor non-profit groups, and for-profit entities closely associated with a charity will likely see a boost in page ranking and online presence.

Measuring Employee Morale

Several years have passed since the creative, 55-person architectural and engineering firm of ARCNET, which specializes in the retail and telecommunications industries, approached our firm with the inevitably cyclical challenge of finding talented and highly skilled staff. The company was spending approximately $1 million each year in human-resource advertising and headhunters' fees to find *the right* people. Growing aggressively and eager to pursue highly qualified employees, ARCNET began offering BMW automobiles to its most creative architects and engineers. Although it was not a cause-marketing effort, the unprecedented BMW giveaways nonetheless generated over 1.5 billion media impressions within 90 days, making ARCNET a household name within the architect and engineer telecom pipelines.

To solidify its position as an employer of choice, the highly visible ARCNET then partnered with Habitat for Humanity. Though its profile was already established, Habitat for Humanity had not yet been adopted as a cause within the architect/engineer community. With our help, ARCNET and Habitat for Humanity executed several media events which included not only staff volunteerism but also activities during which the firm's principals rolled up their sleeves and worked alongside their staff. Both the print and the broadcast media repeatedly interviewed the ARCNET staff at all levels, from company executives to employee volunteers. Infused with a sense of purpose, ARCNET employees spread positive energy and the feelings became contagious. With increasing numbers of their engineers and architects jumping aboard the efforts, the cause-marketing program reached the pinnacle of corporate visibility.

This innovative morale-boosting program cost ARCNET valuable time (not to mention the dollars spent on the BMW giveaways), yet it saved the company $600,000 annually as résumés poured in from around the world. The company's need to pay advertising and headhunter fees was quickly eliminated. Due to its unique benefits package and partnership with Habitat for Humanity, the firm was able to recruit and retain a highly skilled work force.

On the other end of the spectrum is a North Carolina manufacturing company that assembles various textile components made in China. With 28,000 workers, most of whom earned little more than minimum wage, the company's 33-percent turnover was shockingly high, far exceeding the already dismal national industry average of 19 percent. Subsequent training costs were crippling. Making matters worse, employees felt disengaged, and job satisfaction was at an all-time low. Productivity, which is often related to pay scale and job description, was sub-par. When the CEO approached us, he said, "Employees are on automatic pilot but not going at maximum speed."

After evaluating the situation and conducting a cause audit, we were ready to implement a cause-marketing campaign and turn things around. The company CEO was hesitant, saying that the cause-marketing effort did not seem worth the investment. How can an employer with lowly paid, easily replaced workers in a business-to-business environment partner with a charity to increase employee morale? We showed him the math.

The company spent approximately $2,166 per employee for initial training. This included about 240 hours, or three weeks each, of combined salary paid to the trainer and trainee who, during the training period, provided little (if any) production. In addition to this cost, which the client estimated at $1,776 per new employee (240 hours multiplied by a $7.40 average hourly wage), the indirect costs associated with replacing an employee, which included advertising in the daily and weekly newspapers, human-resources processing, etc., was approximately $390 per new employee.

To replace 924 employees (33 percent of 2,800 employees), the company spent over $2 million.

The cause-marketing program which we suggested paired the manufacturing company with an education and literacy non-profit group whose constituents were largely part of an underserved, disadvantaged Hispanic community. Under the partnership, the company's staff would donate 1,000 man-hours per month as volunteers of the non-profit entity, which amounted to approximately 20 minutes per employee per month.

At the time, the average employee earned $7.40 per hour, the equivalent of a $7,400 donation per month in volunteer hours. In addition, the company decided to give a dollar-for-dollar match, bringing the total commitment to $14,800 a month, or $177,600 annually. Let's see how the cost compares to the benefit.

Annually, the company would have to spend $177,600 on its cause-marketing efforts, yet if it could decrease turnover from 33 percent to 16 percent, the company's cost of replacing employees would be reduced to approximately $970,000 instead of $2 million.

Before	**After**
33-percent turnover on 2,800 workers	16-percent turnover on 2,800 workers
924 replacement employees per year	480 replacement employees per year
$2 million replacement cost	$970,000 replacement cost
$0 spent on cause marketing	$177,600 spent on cause marketing
$2 million price tag	$1,147,600 million price tag—an $852,400 savings!

By implementing a cause-marketing program, the company would markedly improve employee turnover, shaving about $852,400 off its direct costs. Two years after implementation, we expect employee turnover to drop even further below industry standards, making the total savings approximately $1 million.

Not worth the investment? The numbers prove otherwise. Aside from the $852,400 per year in savings, the intangible shift in employee morale can make daily work not only bearable but also exciting—a benefit that cannot be calculated in dollar terms.

Employee morale (whether up or down) changes the environment of a corporation. A lack of drive can make the workday miserable, with employees watching the seconds slowly tick away. Measured as much by the company's emotional environment as by quantitative results, heightened morale can be sensed.

Almost always, a cause-marketing campaign changes the corporate culture by making an employee's workday seem less tedious. Management starts to see a shift in the attitude of its workers, who grumble less and work harder. Employees are less frustrated by their jobs. Office politics and gossip diminish and recruitment of qualified professionals becomes easier.

Though the shift in employee spirit is often obvious, this change in the quality of work life also can be measured in the quantitative terms expressed above. A successful cause-marketing campaign measurably results in fewer sick days, lower turnover, and higher reported job satisfaction.

Sick and Personal Days

Based on the Department of Labor's estimate that the average cost of employing an American is about $20 per hour, a company with 50 employees who take an average of eight sick days per year pays $64,000 in sick-leave salary. Reduce this figure by 10 percent and the company can save $6,400. Reduce it by 50% and save $32,000.

Though sick and personal days do have their benefits (mainly, they provide employees with an opportunity to recuperate, and they are usually mandated by law), excessive sick leave can be costly. Although most companies present sick leave as a "just in case" measure, studies show that many employees take advantage of 100 percent of their paid sick-leave days, indicating that workers use these days to take care of personal business, to take the day off, or for extended paid vacations. Employees who are bored with work or who want to schedule an extra vacation often rely on sick leave to skip out on their work duties, especially during summer and around the holidays.

Challenging an employee's use of sick leave and personal days can send an already disgruntled work force over the edge. Accusing an employee of sick-leave abuse is tantamount to accusing an employee of lying, which is not a popular move in a company already lacking in employee morale, especially if the accusation is unaccompanied by proof. And yet, near-perfect attendance improves productivity rates and increases a company's bottom line. With a cause-marketing program in place, a company can see a direct correlation between a successful campaign and a decrease in sick days. Employees are less likely to burn out. They are more likely to *want* to work. Imagine, for instance, how much happier your employees will be if they know that Friday afternoons are devoted to supporting a worthy cause.

Analyzing a change in your company's sick leave is simple. Before kicking off the campaign, calculate the average number of sick days per employee in the past 12 months. One year later, calculate the average again. Conservatively, we can expect to see at least a 10-percent decrease in employee sick leave over the first six months, though this number might be more drastic based on current morale.

Turnover

Turnover costs can be hard to calculate, even in a down economy. Aside from the hard costs, newspaper ads, headhunter fees, moving allowances, and the like necessary to find the right employees, corporations also spend money on indirect costs related to new workers. Trainer and trainee time and related productivity costs are harder to determine, as is the replacement cost of knowledge lost when a seasoned employee walks out the door to start a competitive business from home.

In the worst-case scenarios, turnover can cost an employer up to 200 percent of the employee's annual salary, or $60,000 to replace a worker who makes $30,000. Likely, it will cost at least 25 percent of the employee's salary—$7,500 for the $30,000-a-year employee—in direct and indirect costs, a figure that can be adjusted up or down depending on the industry and region. Consider that replacing a key employee requires top management, who presumably bring in the most business, to sacrifice their time and to devote valuable hours in finding the right replacement. In addition to the time lost interviewing candidates, companies must spend money on recruitment (headhunter fees and advertising). Once a new employee has been hired, seasoned employees must then devote their time to training the new recruit. Sometimes the company also spends money on new technology, relocation costs, signing bonuses or incentives, and the cost of setting up benefits. This doesn't take into account the disruption in workflow and loss of corporate memory that is a natural consequence of losing an employee.

So how much turnover is considered normal? The U.S. Department of Labor found that a 23.4-percent annual turnover in employees was the norm prior to the recession; this statistic varies drastically based upon the specific industry as well as the overall economy. For instance, in the Education and Health Services industry, the annual turnover was 13.5 percent. In the Accommodation and Food Services industry, the turnover was a whopping 56.4 percent (though I have heard of restaurants with a turnover rate of 200 percent!). In today's environment, the annual turnover is more likely to be 3 or 4 percent.

Translated into real dollars, again using the $20/hour assumptions, a 50-person company with a 23.4-percent turnover rate loses almost $122,000 each year as a result. During a down economy, this amount might be closer to $20,000 as turnover will likely be quite low. Keep in mind, though, that this turnover comes at a time when most companies cannot afford extra expenditures.

Either way, upon analyzing your financial records, these figures might seem modest. Your company's unique employee-turnover goals should consider the industry standard, your company's turnover history, and other economic influencers, such as the current unemployment rate and industry-specific factors. We expect to see a turnover rate decline to below national standards as a result of a strong cause-marketing effort.

Keep in mind that achieving a zero-percent turnover rate is not realistic and probably not even desirable. As Jim Collins, author of *Good to Great* says, "If you have the right people on the bus, the problem of how to motivate and manage people largely goes away. The right people don't need to be tightly managed or fired up; they will be self-motivated by the inner drive to produce the best results and to be part of creating something great. If you have the wrong people, it doesn't matter whether you discover the right direction; you *still* won't have a great company. Great vision without great people is irrelevant."

We've all heard that we should "shave off the bottom 10 percent (the underperformers) each year," meaning that, in order to grow a business, we must be constantly improving the overall quality of our bottommost performers, which, in turn, increases our productivity standards. My point here is that it is important to strive to set an attrition-goal rate well beneath the industry standard while at the same time realizing that employee turnover is a fact of doing business and can often be turned into a positive feature.

This being said, in manufacturing and other industrial work environments, strategies to fire up people enough to boost their production can be few and far between. Regardless of their skill set, most workers become bored with tedious, factory-line jobs. In addition to the tried and true "open-book management" practices championed by visionaries such as Jack Stack, a cause-marketing campaign can mean the difference between talented but listless workers and an enthusiastic, devoted work force.

Employee Satisfaction

For a more direct measure of employee morale, companies can conduct anonymous surveys of their employees to measure variables such as job satisfaction and productivity. Such assessments serve as an evaluation of the cause-marketing efforts by directly monitoring the outcomes in terms of employee morale. Feedback can then be used to improve the program activities, address weaknesses, and verify that the cause-marketing program is maintaining its originally planned objectives—in this case, employee morale.

Professional surveying companies can help you develop and administer your company's survey, or you can take a less formal approach by designing your own. Regardless of who compiles and presents the questionnaire, disseminate an anonymous survey asking your employees to measure their job satisfaction. Collect the first set of results prior to kicking off your cause-marketing campaign.

Six months into the campaign, distribute the same survey to the same set of employees. How do your results compare? Note that the most effective way to measure a shift in perception is to conduct the same employee survey four or five times over the course of two or three years.

Remember that your objectives should be measurable, so you might want to set specific goals with respect to your employee-satisfaction survey. For instance, we ask our employees to rate the following statements on a scale of one to ten, with *one* being *I strongly disagree* and *ten* meaning *I strongly agree.*

My job is meaningful.
The company genuinely cares.

We then average the answers to these survey questions, and consider anything above a seven to be a success. The following page has a sample survey designed to gauge employee satisfaction.

Survey #1: Employee Satisfaction Survey

Which of the following adjectives would you use to describe the management?

- ☐ Cold
- ☐ Compassionate
- ☐ Fair
- ☐ Manipulative
- ☐ Closed-minded
- ☐ Charitable
- ☐ Unwilling to listen

Rate the following statements on a scale of one to ten, with one being I strongly disagree and ten meaning I strongly agree.

- ☐ I am satisfied with my job.
- ☐ My job is meaningful.
- ☐ Management listens to my concerns.
- ☐ My at-work interactions are positive.
- ☐ I am fairly compensated.
- ☐ The benefits plan is competitive.
- ☐ I am unlikely to search for another job.
- ☐ I work in a supportive environment.
- ☐ My employer cares about me and the community.
- ☐ My co-workers are enthusiastic.
- ☐ I go the extra mile to be productive.

Recruitment

Asking about a company's social programs and digging more deeply have become commonplace among interviewees, especially those candidates who are positioned for management careers. Now more than ever, in our complex modern world, employees are concerned whether the companies for which they work are addressing social issues through charitable involvement. They deduce that, if the company is to be compassionate and community-minded, it must also be mindful of its people. A company that incorporates a socially responsible agenda into its employee-benefits package is considered to be more competitive and more appealing. As such, a properly executed cause-marketing effort should increase both the quality and quantity of applicants to a company as it strives to increase brand awareness. Indeed, a 2004 survey found that a company with a reputation as a strong corporate citizen should see a 4-percent increase in its number of applicants.[30]

Recruitment efforts can be measured both in terms of the number of potential employees interested in working for your company, as well as the quality of these employees. Measuring quantity is easy, but quality can also be addressed through simple strategies, though often less objective. Businesses can also gauge the ease of recruitment by ranking the eventual workers based on desirability. Did the company hire its first-choice or fifth-choice candidate? In addition, a clear indicator that your employee relations are strong occurs when employees start referring their friends, family members, and colleagues to fill open positions.

Remembering to take both "before" and "during" measurements, a company can score the desirability of the top 20 candidates for a position on a scale of one to ten, comparing outcomes as the cause-marketing program progresses.

Managing or Avoiding Crises

Using similar surveys described earlier, both internal and external studies can be undertaken to gauge perception from employees, the general public, or past and present business partners. We call this a "Perception Rating" and we implement survey tools that allow our clients to ascertain their perception rating from each stakeholder. After all, perception is reality.

Employee Perception Rating

To gauge an employee's perception of a company, we use Survey #1 from the previous pages, averaging the results into one score. A perception rating of seven or above is considered strong, though we aim for an eight or higher.

Customer-Base Perception Rating

We want our clients' potential customer base not only to know about the company (brand awareness) but also to have a strongly favorable opinion of the company. To determine the public's perception of a company, especially a company that is fighting to regain its reputation after a crisis, we suggest hiring a research company to estimate how the public views that particular floundering company. Survey tools can easily be tailored for geographical relevance, such as public perception of the company locally, nationally, or even globally, thus allowing companies to better understand where to focus their cause-marketing efforts in order to maximize their return on investment.

However, the general public is less likely to agree to engage in lengthy surveys than are employees, who can be required to fill out their "Perception Rating" survey. To ensure that the survey is hassle-free, easy, and quick, we use a simple three-question survey:

1) Have you heard of [Company X]?
   If the survey participant has never heard of the company, we thank the respondent and move on. If yes, we move forward to question two.

2) Is your opinion of [Company X] good, bad, or neutral?
   If neutral, this answer is not scored or considered in the final score.

3) If [Company X] sold a product or service which you wanted or needed, would you consider conducting business with [Company X]?

The scoring model is simple. For the second and third questions, affirmative responses are scored with a one, while answers to the negative are given a zero. From this, we average the points assigned to questions two and three. We then calculate the average of all responses, assuming a 0.7 or higher to be favorable.

We suggest that clients, regardless of whether or not they are in a crisis, know their perception rating as it relates to stakeholders, customers, business partners, and any other audience important to them. When and if a crisis occurs that could affect a group's opinion of a company, the company has a benchmark from which it can gauge the efficacy, positive or negative, of future public relations efforts. If the employee perception rating of your corporation is a seven and it falls to three after a crisis, your goal is to engage in a cause-marketing campaign that moves the score back toward seven or above.

If the first page of a Google search results in negative information about your company pursuant to a crisis, then you should act rapidly to create cause-related news stories that can help combat and replace those stories, blogs, and news items. Online reputation management relies on fresh content, social media, and online news to dominate the pages on Google, Bing, and Yahoo.

Creating a Fresh Publicity Strategy

A successful cause-marketing relationship builds a lasting relationship, not just between a non-profit entity and a corporation but also among the partnership and the media. Ongoing publicity means that the collaboration always remains fresh in the eye of the public. Measuring a campaign's publicity results is fairly straightforward.

How many media impressions has a company received as a result of its cause partnership? Media impressions are based on the readership of a newspaper or magazine, number of visitors to a website, the number of viewers of a particular television show, or listeners to the radio station on which your cause-marketing partnership is promoted. If a cause-marketing campaign receives coverage on a local television news show with an audience of 432,000 as well as in a newspaper with a 900,000-person readership, and online visibility of 500,000, the cause partnership has generated 1.832 million media impressions. Media coverage is not the end all and be all, but nobody argues against the benefits of sustained visibility!

Keep in mind that saturating a geographic area with a message helps to build awareness and change opinion. Therefore, media placements should be intentional, numerous (in layers), and ongoing in order to effect the most positive outcome.

A campaign's success in attaining ongoing publicity can also be measured by the number of inquiries which a partnership receives from its media coverage. Using your website to measure interest and action greatly helps you to determine the impact of the program. Then, go one step further and re-purpose the media placements, using them as third-party endorsements and selling tools. This improves credibility and can influence your various target audiences. Send them regularly to anyone who buys or sells your products or services.

What If Your Efforts Are Unsuccessful?

We recently began working with a client who had previously implemented a cause-marketing partnership without outside assistance. It failed, and the client quickly gave up. Because its kickoff had been a failure, attracting not a single media outlet, the company had not seen any return on its investment. Therefore, it was not the least bit interested in resurrecting the campaign. Nonetheless, we reviewed the client's press materials and quickly realized why it had failed to evoke a response or interest. The kickoff was held on a less-than-desirable day at an inconvenient time for the media, and the company's s media alert was dull and lacked good photo ops.

We convinced the client to give it one more shot, this time with outside counsel. We re-wrote their media advisory, included a strong photo, and re-executed the launch. The result? We landed one national television placement, three local network affiliates, the largest daily paper in the region, a weekly newspaper, a half dozen of the most prominent trade publications in the industry, and more than 200 online placements—all due to a 25-minute press event, sound strategies, and proper execution.

Feedback into why a campaign is not working can be simple, and smart strategists or media consultants can help you determine the culprit of a failed cause-marketing campaign. Typically, an unsuccessful campaign stems from a lackluster overall strategy, though the details of this strategy should also be considered. News releases might be too long or might not be written in a style that demands the media's attention. Perhaps you are not spending sufficient time contacting the media. Have you neglected the all-too-important photo op? Did you overlook the AP Day Book? Some corporations make the mistake of sending one media advisory and then giving up when the media fails to respond. Remember to layer your communication with media outlets and follow up tenaciously. (Repetition is the mother of all learning.)

Perception Rating: On a measurable scale, the reputation of a business as determined by a stakeholder, customer, business partner, potential customer, or employee.

If the media simply are not biting despite all the above efforts, try asking a reporter or editor why the media are not covering your event.

Likewise, before pulling the plug on a cause-marketing campaign designed to attract higher quality employees, try asking favored candidates what would make the job opportunity more competitive. If employee morale is low, submit an anonymous survey asking employees to offer suggestions about improving quality of work. You might find that only one manager who is ill-suited for his job is causing low employee morale throughout your company.

Asking for feedback may seem contrary to the nature of a company positioning itself for success. Most corporate leaders consider self-assurance to be at the heart of their ability to expand, and

Saturating a geographic area with a message helps to build awareness and change opinion; therefore, media placements should be intentional, numerous (in layers), and ongoing in order to effect the most positive outcome.

they may feel that asking for feedback will be interpreted by their employees as a sign of weakness or uncertainty. It isn't. Asking for feedback can save a company time, energy, and frustration. If you ask your customers and employees what they want, your cause-marketing campaign will be better positioned to succeed.

Remember, change and growth take time. If you do not see the results you anticipated within three months of initiating your campaign, it may be premature to pull the plug on the partnership. Give a campaign six months to seep into the media and your customers' consciousness to create the desired result. However, the effort should begin generating results within the first 45 days of its initial implementation.

Make sure, as well, that the less-than-favorable outcomes are not because of another economic factor. Determine exactly what isn't working, and try to ascertain what influences are affecting the company. If your company is experiencing lackluster sales, for instance, is it because the economy as a whole has taken a downturn or is the cause-marketing campaign not doing its job?

Would the company be in even worse shape if it hadn't executed the campaign in the first place?

Conclusion:

The Cause & Effect Of Cause Marketing

In a cause-marketing campaign, much emphasis is always given to the corporation's bottom line. That a cause-marketing partnership is driven by profit-related objectives is what separates it from simple donations and makes it a strategy rather than a duty. Though perhaps not the only one, profit is a corporate responsibility and most, if not all, CEOs would consider it to be the most important one. It should steer the cause-marketing program, influencing the objectives, the partner selection, and the partnership's parameters and activities.

Yet I must admit that the correlating outcomes are often the most rewarding. As an almost necessary consequence, a cause-marketing agenda changes the corporate culture of a business. As Val Halamandaris, founder of the National Association for Home Care and Hospice, said about home care, compassion and efficiency are not mutually exclusive. While the business will (and should) remain profit-driven, upon engaging in a cause-marketing effort, it begins to recognize that business and compassion can exist side by side.

Under an effective cause-marketing program, all team members begin to find more meaning in their jobs. They become more engaged. The work environment becomes fun and energized. Employee morale increases despite staffing fluctuations and increases in workload. A common ground is developed between employee and employer as the two begin to embrace each other's goals.

A cause-marketing campaign opens up a company's heart. Everyone—from top management to seasonal help—begins seeing the positive changes the partnership is effecting in the community. And then, dare I say, they begin to see that they can impact the world.

* * * * * * * * *

Notes

The Case for Cause Marketing

[1] Ortlizky, Mark, Frank L. Schmidt, and Sara L. Rynes. "Corporate Social and Financial Performance: A Meta-Analysis." *Organization Studies* 24 (2003): 403-441, http://www.finanzasostenibile.it/finanza/moskowitz2004.pdf.

[2] Deloitte & Touche. *Deloitte Survey Reveals That 72 Percent of Americans Want to Work for Companies That Support Charitable Causes.* New York: Harris Interactive, October 6, 2004.

[3] Garcia, Tonya. "The Spirit of Generosity." *PRWeek*, October 22, 2007, http://www.prweekus.com/pages/login.aspx?returl=/the-spirit-of-generosity/article/58036/&pagetypeid=28&articleid=58036&accesslevel=2&expireddays=0&accessAndPrice=0

[4] Cone Inc. *Cone Corporate Citizen Study: Building Brand Trust.* Massachusetts: Cone Inc., 2004.

[5] U.S. Small Business Administration. *Small Business Profile: New Jersey.* Washington DC: Office of Advocacy, 2004, http://www.sba.gov/advo/stats/profiles/04nj.pdf.

[6] Csikszentmihalyi, Mihaly. Flow: *The Psychology of Optimal Experience.* New York: Harper and Row, 1990.

[7] National Federation of Independent Business. *The Seven Times Factor.* Tennessee: Business Toolbox 2002, http://www.nfib.com/object/1611470.html.

[8] Richman, Dan. "Giving Away Microsoft's Millions." *Seattle Post-Intelligence Reporter*, June 12, 2001, http://seattlepi.nwsource.com/business/27032_brooks12.shtml.

[9] Glosserman, Phil and Larry Pinci. *Sell the Feeling: The 6-Step System that Drives People to Do Business with You.* New York: Morgan James Publishing, 2008.

[10] Friedman, Milton. "The Social Responsibility of Business Is to Increase Its Profits," *The New York Times Magazine*, September 13, 1970.

[11] Friedman Milton, John Mackey, and T.J. Rodgers, "Rethinking the Social Responsibility of Business." *Reason*, October 2005.

[12] Cone Inc. *Cone Corporate Citizen Study: Building Brand Trust.* Massachusetts: Cone Inc., 2004.

[13] Friedman Milton, John Mackey, and T.J. Rodgers, "Rethinking the Social Responsibility of Business." *Reason*, October 2005.

[14] Cone Inc. *Cone Corporate Citizen Study: Building Brand Trust.* Massachusetts: Cone Inc., 2004.

[15] Muirhead, Sophia. "Philanthropy and Business: The Changing Agenda." The Conference Board, May 2006.

Notes

Identifying Your Objectives

[16] Cone Inc. *Cone Corporate Citizen Study: Building Brand Trust.* Massachusetts: Cone Inc., 2004.

[17] Stavraka, Carol. "Want Loyal Employees? Try Supporting Social Issues." *Diversity Inc. Magazine*, September 26, 2000, http://www.diversityinc.com.

[18] LaPlante, Alice. "MBA Graduates Want to Work for Caring and Ethical Employees." *Stanford GSB News*, January 2004, http://www.gsb.stanford.edu/news/research/hr_mbajobchoice.shtml.

[19] "Employee Monitoring Statistics." *Computer Monitoring*, http://www.computer-monitoring.com/employee-monitoring/stats.htm.

[20] Grodzinsky, Frances S. and Andra Gumbus. "Internet and Productivity: Ethical Perspectives on Workplace Behavior." *Internet, Communications and Ethics in Society 3* (2006): 249-256.

[21] Moses, Barbara. "The Mid-Career Lament: 'I'm Bored.'" *The Globe and Mail*, October 21, 2005, http://www.theglobeandmail.com/report-on-business/the-mid-career-lament-im-bored/article347013.

[22] Adams, Cecil. "Is the Chinese Word for 'Crisis' a Combination of 'Danger' and 'Opportunity'?" *The Straight Dope*, November 3, 2000, http://www.straightdope.com/columns/read/2363/is-the-chinese-word-for-crisis-a-combination-of-danger-and-opportunity.

[23] It bears noting here that the Stew Leonard's case study breaks one of *The Cause Marketing Handbook's* cardinal rules: Own one primary charity. In this case, the wishing well presented a singular theme, so we made an exception.

Conducting A Casue Marketing Audit and Choosing A Cause Partner

[24] Whole Foods Market. *Whole Foods Market Fourth Quarter Results.* Texas: Whole Foods Market, November 4, 2009.

[25] Bethune, Gordon. *From Worst to First: Behind the Scenes of Continental's Remarkable Comeback.* John Wiley & Sons, May 1999.

[26] Zimmerman, Jennifer. "Motivating Employees Is Key to Success, According to Continental Airlines CEO." *Stanford GSB News*, May 2001, http://www.gsb.stanford.edu/news/headlines/bethune.shtml.

[27] Garcia, Tonya. "The Spirit of Generosity." *PRWeek*, October 22, 2007, http://www.prweekus.com/pages/login.aspx?returl=/the-spirit-of-generosity/article/58036/&pagetypeid=28&articleid=58036&accesslevel=2&expireddays=0&accessAndPrice=0

[28] Muolo, Paul. "Letter to the Editor." *Columbia Journalism Review*, March/April 2002.

[29] Incidentally, ribbons are passé and seldom noticed today. The red ribbon signifies the fight against AIDS; the white ribbon stands against violence toward women; the yellow ribbon symbolizes support for active military troops; and, of course, the pink ribbon is a sign for breast-cancer awareness. They are merely a symbol, and an overused one at that, raising barely any money for the people in need, though gas stations around the country seem to benefit from the sale of ribbons supporting various causes.

Measuring Results

[30] Cone Inc. *Cone Corporate Citizen Study: Building Brand Trust.* Massachusetts: Cone Inc., 2004.

About the author:

Christopher Rosica
CEO, Rosica Communications
Author, The Authentic Brand

Christopher Rosica, CEO of Rosica Communications, is a recognized public relations and marketing expert, speaker, and author. He is passionate about entrepreneurship and helping businesses grow, adapt to change, outpace the competition, and improve internal and external communications. Rosica's national PR firm serves a variety of industries and specializes in media relations, message development, cause-related marketing, crisis communications/planning, and online marketing as a means of building brand awareness. An authority on cause marketing, Rosica also authored *The Business of Cause Marketing: Doing Well By Doing Good* (Noble Press), which details the process and effects of incorporating cause marketing into a company's business and promotional agenda. He is a frequent keynote speaker, media trainer, and public-speaking coach who teaches CEOs, salespeople, corporate and non-profit executives, and college students. Rosica has lectured at Fordham, Seton Hall and PACE universities and numerous other colleges and universities in the NY metro area. As part of a symposium for the Young Presidents' Organization (YPO) and the Entrepreneurs' Organization (EO), Rosica received high accolades for his interview with renowned CEO Jack Welch. Rosica is past president of New York's Young Entrepreneurs' Organization (YEO), chairs the public relations committee for EO Global, and serves on several non-profit boards, including Boys & Girls Clubs in New Jersey. In 2006, he completed the "Birthing of Giants," an exclusive three-year course on entrepreneurship at MIT sponsored by EO in conjunction with Inc. Magazine and the MIT Enterprise Forum. He recently completed the Leadership New Jersey curriculum, which connects the state's corporate, governmental, and non-profit leaders to affect positive change. Rosica is a graduate of Florida International and Johnson & Wales Universities; he lives in New Jersey with his wife, Wendy, daughter, and son.